J LOREN

5

**SOLID ROCK
CHRISTIAN
FELLOWSHIP**

BATTLE STRATEGIES
OF A
VICTORIOUS WARRIOR

ISBN-13: 978-0692825563
ISBN-10: 0692825568

TELL IT LIKE IT IS, INC.

CONTENTS

Repent   97

Forgive   147

Forget   175

INTRODUCTION

A snap, a sound, a glance backward, an unexpected noise. Wait. Nothing. Only a few more steps to the prize… Then a light, a blinding light, brighter than the morning sun filled the room with a rush like giant wings. She looked at him with a loving but painful stare. "If you turn that thing back on to look at those pictures so help me, it's over." And the demons of lust fled in fright as the angels of God filled the room with a warm and tender cry. The crisis of truth had come. Another demonic attack is averted.

Everyday, in homes all over the world a battle rages. Those homes are mansions on the hills outside of Los Angeles, they are cardboard shelters on the streets of Dallas, they are huts in the villages of the Congo, palatial estates in the jungles outside Medellin, Colombia and slums of Rio De Janeiro, Brazil.

Those homes are filled with hurting hearts ravaged by poor choices and believed lies. Too many families have been ripped apart by the deception of selfishness, the want for more, a belief this world is all mine for the taking. From drugs, to money laundering, from pornography and prostitution to gang violence and sex trafficking of minors, the fallen nature of mankind has left a path of destruction for centuries across this globe.

What happens when we surrender to our own selfish desires? What happens when the "natural cravings" we are born with are not brought under the mastery of self-control? What happens when a natural desire becomes an addiction? Pain! Destruction! Destroyed relationships! Broken hearts and broken homes! Incarceration! Death! When natural cravings become addictions, you become a slave to cravings. I know because it happened to me.

For the first ten years of my marriage I put my wife through hell because of the addiction I brought to our wedding day. In the eleventh year we began to fight, no longer face to face, now back to back. Looking out for each other, we fought to save our marriage and find victory over my addiction. Sexual addiction and pornography were my slave master for more than two decades, but they are no more.

Perhaps you picked up this book because you wanted to study spiritual warfare. Perhaps someone gave it to you because you are already engaged in spiritual warfare fighting for your family, your freedom or even your life. Perhaps your addiction is wealth, power, influence, sex, drugs, alcohol, tobacco, control, rage or food. It does not matter. If it is an addiction, you are the slave, not the master. I promise you, this slave master has only one intention: TO DESTROY YOU!

Through the pages of this book I will share some direct details about my battle with addiction. DO NOT believe the lie your mind will try to force on you. It will be easy to say,

"Well, that is not the craving I have, so that is not my problem" or, "That solution may work for his addiction, but it won't work for mine." Your enemy and mine are the same. Your slave master and mine have the same origin, the same name and the same agenda. My habits may have been different. My cravings may have been different. My consequences may have been different. But the enemy of your soul is the enemy of mine.

"If it is an addiction, you are the slave, not the master. I promise you, this slave master has only one intention: TO DESTROY YOU!"

If you will trust me on this journey through the back woods of your mind, through the dark caverns of your heart, into the recesses of your soul, I will point you toward and introduce you to the biggest, baddest warrior you have ever met. He will literally scare the hell right out of your life. Every demon who calls your name in the night, every spirit who haunts your nightmares, every dark whisper which draws your attention to destructive cravings and damaging behavior knows this warrior by name, and they tremble with fear at the sight of Him.

If you are ready to fight your addiction, and believe I can lead you in the right direction, keep reading. This book is going to get intense, direct and merciless for awhile, but it will lead to the light, the peace, and the hope you have been seeking.

If you are brave enough to follow the instructions you are about to read, you will find freedom here. He is waiting and He is calling you by name.

If your life has been ravaged by thoughts, behaviors and attitudes which bring about more pain than promise, you are holding the right book. Do not put it down. That is exactly what the slave master wants. Now is not the time to get brave on your own. Now is not the time to cower and hide. Now is not the time to put off this confrontation for one more season, month, week, day or hour. NOW IS THE TIME TO FIGHT FOR YOUR FREEDOM!!

TACTICS TO WIN

The action or strategy carefully planned to achieve a specific end. The art of disposing armed forces in the order of battle, especially during contact with an enemy.

WE AGREE

Failure in relationships, dreams destroyed in an instant, all the hope of the future snatched away and dashed upon the rocks, this is the repeated experience of every addict. Just when you think you have this monkey off your back, just when you have declared victory and shook your fist in the face of your bondage it slaps you to the ground again in mockery.

Nothing is more demoralizing than falling prey to a weakness. Nothing rips your heart out more than knowing you have tasted victory and defeat in the same moment. Nothing leaves you more hopeless than the look of pain in your best friend's eye when you realize they too no longer believe you care enough to win this battle.

I am not drawing any comparison to which addictions are worse. The slave master of addiction will use whichever ropes, chains, stocks or hot irons will do the trick for the day. The slave master knows from generations of experience what will break you and seems to get some sadistic joy in applying the punishment.

My slave master was sexual addiction. Yours may be alcohol, drugs, work, narcissism, food, money or control. It doesn't really matter. When you are a slave, you do what you're told.

Over the next several sections of this book I will dig into the parallels between your addiction and mine. I will reveal some painful moments of my past, I will challenge you to confront yours.

When you reach the end of this book you will be empowered in a way like never before to stare down your slave master with bold confidence and demand your freedom. You will find hope of restoration, power to forgive, humility to ask for forgiveness and courage to face the consequences.

THE ENEMY WITHIN

This book is laced with scriptural references and Bible quotations. Don't let that scare you. You are reading this because what you have tried up to now has failed. It is time to apply some deeper wisdom. You don't know what you don't know. That's what a mentor is for. That's what learning is for.

In order for you to find victory over bondage, you must first admit to some basic truths.

What you are:

1. You are born of the flesh and will by nature crave the things of the flesh.

2. You are by nature created with a longing for sexual attention, attraction and satisfaction.

3. You are by nature selfish, self-centered and self-absorbed.

4. You are by nature prideful.

5. You are by nature capable of some degree of self-control.

6. You are by nature incapable of perfection.

What you are not:

1. You are NOT naturally inclined to walk away from pleasurable things.

2. You are NOT naturally inclined to ignore the cravings or desires of your body.

3. You are NOT naturally inclined to think of others first.

4. You are NOT naturally inclined to being humble.

5. You are NOT naturally inclined to seek after holiness.

6. You are NOT naturally inclined to perform the will of God.

    "Now the works of the flesh are evident: sexual immorality, impurity, sensuality, idolatry, sorcery, enmity, strife, jealousy, fits of anger, rivalries, dissensions, divisions, envy, drunkenness, orgies, and things like these. I warn you, as I warned you before, that those who do such things will not inherit the kingdom of God."
    Galatians 5:19-21 ESV http://bible.com/59/gal. 5.19-21.esv

Dogs bark, cats meow and birds fly. I have never seen a dog fly about the heavens of its own accord. It is not natural. What is the nature of you? What part of you is the natural you? The sinful part of you is natural. You are born after the nature of Adam.

"Therefore, just as sin came into the world through one man, and death through sin, and so death spread to all men because all sinned— for sin indeed was in the world before the law was given, but sin is not counted where there is no law."
Romans 5:12-13 ESV http://bible.com/59/rom.5.12-13.esv
"For as by the one man's disobedience the many were made sinners, so by the one man's obedience the many will be made righteous."
Romans 5:19 ESV http://bible.com/59/rom.5.19.esv

The flesh part of you which you are born with is corrupt. The heart is deceitfully wicked. You might think you can trust your heart, but you can't. You might think you know right from wrong, but naturally speaking, you can do nothing about it. It is not in you, if you walk after the flesh, to resist the evil desires when they present themselves to you.

When we talk about sin, there are two very real enemies. One is the nature within you. The other is the enemy of your soul. Satan, Lucifer, the Deceiving Father of Lies, the Old Dragon who wants only to kill, to steal and to destroy.

Satan knows the game of Spiritual Warfare much better than we do. You could not likely score a three pointer on Michael Jordan or out putt Tiger Woods, nor will you in your own ability out think, out strategize or out maneuver Satan. He is wily, hate filled and bent on your demise. He has all the time in the world to wait for your moment of weakness. He has all the demons of Hell at his beck and call. He has unseen power beyond human imagination and worst of all, he actually has some human devotees who are influenced by his will and surrendered to his service.

No, if you want to get one up on the Old Dragon, you need help. You need a playbook where all his tricks are exposed. You need an all-star team for back-up. You will need an unstoppable offense and a tireless unbeatable defense. What you need is the King of Kings and his legion of Angels. You need His Word.

> "Finally, be strong in the Lord and in the strength of his might. Put on the whole armor of God, that you may be able to stand against the schemes of the devil. For we do not wrestle against flesh and blood, but against the rulers, against the authorities, against the cosmic powers over this present darkness, against the spiritual forces of evil in the heavenly places. Therefore take up the whole armor of God, that you may be able to withstand in the evil day, and having done all, to stand firm. Stand therefore, having fastened on the belt of truth, and having put on the breastplate of righteousness, and, as shoes for your feet, having put on the readiness given by the gospel of peace. In all circumstances take up the shield of faith, with which you can extinguish all the flaming darts of the evil one; and take the helmet of salvation, and the sword of the Spirit, which is the word of God,"
> Ephesians 6:10-17 ESV http://bible.com/59/eph.6.10-17.esv

You cannot defeat either enemy on your own. The nature in you will eat you up from the inside and the Dragon will eat you up from the outside. Left unattended, sin will devour you. But keep reading, there is HOPE!

TACTICAL ARENAS

I have discovered in twenty years on the addiction battlefield ten very specific arenas where the battle lines become abundantly clear and very distinct. Through the course of this book, I will expose each of these ten arenas through five very carefully chosen lenses.

The five lenses are: **Identify, Confess, Repent, Forgive and Forget (aka ICRFF)**. These lenses are also five strategies. Like the basics of any sport, you must learn to master each of the five strategies in all ten tactical arenas. Some of these tactics will come easy to you, some will require great effort, intention and discipline. Some of you will quickly and easily master certain tactics and struggle in others, while some will find different tactics easier to master.

This book is broken in to five main sections, one for each strategy. Within each strategy, we will dive deeper into each of the ten tactical arenas and discuss the actions needed to find victory and freedom.

Each tactical arena will require specific action from you in order to master the arena. Each of the five strategies ends with a Summary & Action section for you to reflect and apply what you have learned and to keep notes of the action you have already taken to win the war within.

IDENTIFY

To recognize someone or something for who or what they are is the opposite of denial and the beginning of freedom.

SIN

In the darkness he came, stalking, creeping, and almost imperceptible. The sound of his approach was nothing more than a rustle, the plan was stealthy and the goal utter destruction. He knew he could get caught which only added to the excitement. No one in the universe could understand this craving. Not one soul knew of the unbridled passions which drove his behavior. Should this one last indulgence see the fullness of its own possibilities the result could be DEATH...

It starts as a glance in the closet while dad is off to work. The books become a fascination and everyone who comes to visit has to see them. Then the books are not enough, they have a strange effect on the young body. These images create a desire for the real thing, a look, perhaps at a sibling or relative of the opposite sex in the shower or tub. If this craving cannot be met, perhaps the desire can be met with the others who are viewing and craving too. If two boys have the same craving and they can fulfill each other, why explain that craving to anyone else? Perhaps there won't be any feelings and commitments and "relationships" to mess things up.

In the teenage years, it is always easy to find a willing and curious partner. After all, the ads on TV, the songs on the radio, the clothing ads in the junior section of the catalog all show enough to get the conversation started. Then there is the peer pressure. Isn't everyone doing it already?

As a grown man, there are troubles in store. Suddenly, responsibility and relationships, feelings and emotions complicate what was once simple and instant gratification. Next thing you know, what you crave, she won't consent to. Do you "take it" anyway? Do you walk away dissatisfied? Do you look for someone who will do everything you crave, even if you must pay for it? Where does the cycle stop? How far is too far?

Anyone who has wrestled with any type of addiction knows that what once did the trick, becomes old hat. What was ecstasy last time is boring this time. What was more than I could even consider, becomes something I have to try.

"For the wrath of God is revealed from heaven against all ungodliness and unrighteousness of men, who by their unrighteousness suppress the truth. For what can be known about God is plain to them, because God has shown it to them. For his invisible attributes, namely, his eternal power and divine nature, have been clearly perceived, ever since the creation of the world, in the things that have been made. So they are without excuse. For although they knew God, they did not honor him as God or give thanks to him, but they became futile in their thinking, and their foolish hearts were darkened. Claiming to be wise, they became fools, and exchanged the glory of the immortal God for images resembling mortal man and birds and animals and creeping things. Therefore God gave them up in the lusts of their hearts to impurity, to the dishonoring of their bodies among themselves, because they exchanged the truth about God for a lie and worshiped and served the creature rather than the Creator, who is blessed forever! Amen. For this reason God gave them up to dishonorable passions. For their women exchanged natural relations for those that are contrary to nature; and the men likewise gave up natural relations with women and were consumed with passion for one another, men committing shameless acts with men and receiving in themselves the due penalty for their error. And since they did not see fit to acknowledge God, God gave them up to a debased mind to do what ought not to be done. They were filled with all manner of unrighteousness, evil, covetousness, malice. They are full of envy, murder, strife, deceit, maliciousness. They are gossips, slanderers, haters of God, insolent, haughty, boastful, inventors of evil, disobedient to parents, foolish, faithless, heartless, ruthless. Though they know God's righteous decree that those who practice such things deserve to die, they not only do them but give approval to those who practice them."

Romans 1:18-32 ESV http://bible.com/59/rom.1.18-32.esv

Please know, there is not a man or woman reading this book who has seen the reality of their addiction and comprehended it, who still believes it is victimless. The nature of all other sin is outside the body, but the nature of sexual sin is not. It corrupts from within and destroys all it touches.

Much of my life has been a constant battle. To paraphrase Paul "everything I try to avoid, I end up doing and everything I try to do, just doesn't seem to happen."[1]

It seems to me to be a phenomenon of human psychology, we know the difference between right and wrong. We know wrongdoing has consequences. We know if we do wrong and get caught there will be a high price to pay. The price could be emotional, financial, physical, or even spiritual, but it will be high to be sure.

If we drive too fast we get a ticket. If we don't pay the ticket, we get a warrant. If we don't answer to the warrant we go to jail. But all of these can be avoided by simply obeying traffic laws. It would seem a simple matter then to obey the law.

In the area of addiction, we know the same. Each action has a reaction, each choice an outcome, each decision a consequence. Some of those choices and results are good; others are not.

If I choose to allow myself the indulgences to which I have become accustomed, I find I have new, deeper, more deviant

---

[1] Romans 7:8-12 KJV

cravings. Each time I enjoy the "natural" desires and cravings of the flesh, what was once beyond my imagination becomes an object of desire. What once I could not accept, I now long for.

When I was a teenager, I was a jealous guy. I can remember telling my girlfriend that if I ever caught her with someone else I would beat him to a pulp. I could not bear the thought of "my girl" with someone else. Yet in the depth of my bondage to sexual sin and sexual addiction, I fantasized about the idea of my wife with some other guy. I justified that if she was truly enjoying herself, I could get whatever I wanted out of the deal. The consequence of giving in repeatedly to your addiction is this: **deeper bondage to your addiction.** Do not be fooled, God is not mocked, what ever you sow, you will reap! What goes up, must come down. These are really simple rules.

Steve Gallagher in his book, "At the Altar of Sexual Idolatry"[2] makes a fantastic observation. He concludes that the two root issues of sexual sin are pride and self-centeredness. I agree whole-heartedly. I know I can see the 20/20 hindsight of my own life and attest to this fact. I know when I visit with men and women who struggle with addiction, they are self-absorbed and more often than not filled with an unbelievable amount of pride.

---

[2] http://store.purelifeministries.org/at-the-altar-of-sexual-idolatry

The matter of overcoming addiction has many areas of concern which must be addressed. In this book we will address not only understanding your addiction as sin but also the impact sin has on you, your relationship to others and your relationship to God.

SIN = I will.

When we do not understand the role our relationship to God plays in the existence of the universe it is hard for us to understand the impact sin has on our lives. When I say relationship in this sense I mean like the relationship water has to a boat, a gun to a bullet, a shoe to a shoelace.

Without Him, we have no purpose, no ability to accomplish anything, no chance to bear fruits of success or obedience.[3] We cannot make a day to begin or end.

We cannot so much as take another breath, should He choose otherwise. The magnitude of this reality should be mind-boggling. It should take our breath away. It should make us gasp in awe. His inconceivable love patiently endures our ignorance and pride. And yet we stand defiantly, arrogantly and declare in all authority "Today, I will buy a new car, next month a new home. I will leave my wife to find another who will satisfy me more. I will choose this substance or action and I will... I will... I will."

> "Come now, you who say, "Today or tomorrow we will go into such and such a town and spend a year there and

[3] John 15:5 ESV

trade and make a profit"— yet you do not know what tomorrow will bring. What is your life? For you are a mist that appears for a little time and then vanishes. Instead you ought to say, "If the Lord wills, we will live and do this or that." As it is, you boast in your arrogance. All such boasting is evil. So whoever knows the right thing to do and fails to do it, for him it is sin."
James 4:13-17 ESV http://bible.com/59/jas.4.13-17.esv

Could we not find it in our hearts to seek the guidance of such a thoughtful and benevolent Creator.

Surely you are asking:

"What does this have to do with sexual sin or any other type of addiction?" Selfishness and Pride!

"If we are born with natural desires for food, shelter, and bodily functions, it would seem only right that we be given the liberty by the Almighty to exercise those desires and needs."

"If we are hungry, have we not the right to food?"

"If cold, have we not the right to shelter?"

Of course, God has made a way for all of these. However if I came to your home, ate from your fridge and slept in your bed without permission you might be upset, and I might be a thief.   If I felt the urge to relieve myself while in your swimming pool, you might be inclined to disappointment. Right? The truth is, there are limitations of society and law which allow us to meet the needs of our body, but not at the expense of another.

When was the last time you wet your pants? Unless you are under three years old, or have a bladder condition or other medical problem, you probably have learned enough self-control to wait until it is an appropriate time to relieve yourself. If you have a job and work for someone else, you likely have a scheduled mealtime. You manage to keep your hunger pangs at bay until the appropriate time arrives out of respect for your boss. If these natural urges or cravings and even life necessities can be controlled by your thoughts and the power of your will, how can you expect me to believe the urge for sexual gratification could be beyond your ability to resist? Do you really think the next drink, the next snack, the next hit, the fit of rage is a decision beyond your control?

Who are you to look into the face of the Creator who created you and make demands? Who are you to assume He doesn't understand our passions? Who are you to declare to His creation you should be served, your every desire should be met? What tree did you create from scratch today?

When you cry the laws of sin and death should not apply to you because you are only fulfilling a need God placed in you, when you blame your sinful desires on those who fail to meet them, when you refuse to accept the goodness of God as good enough, you spit in the face of Mercy.

Trample under foot the Love of the Almighty? Nail to a Cross the only begotten Son? Draw from His hands, His feet,

His side, the very lifeblood that spares you from eternal damnation, and then ask for more? Are you insane? As if to say, "Eternity was not enough; I want a better fix - I want more sex - I want more control."

Have I made my point to the point of the ridiculous? Good!

Then you understand what I am telling you clearly: pornography, masturbation, lustful fantasies, fornication, exhibitionism, rape, incest, homosexuality and any other type of behavior outside God's plan is sin. It's not just something men do. It's not just boys being boys. It's not just doing what is natural. It is SIN! When you choose to engage in these behaviors you declare to God, I WILL choose my fleshly desires over your holiness and I WILL choose to fulfill my needs on this earth and not your desires for me.

This is also true of ANY OTHER ADDICTION. Do you crave the next hit more than you crave God? Do you crave the next drink, smoke, bite more than you crave God? Do you wrestle with the idea of God being in control of your life because it means you will not be?

If this is the attitude of your heart, spoken or not, you need to examine your life and your heart right now. There is only one destination for this path. You may live a life for the moment of great joy and frolicking fun. You may sow your wild oats and leave your mark on this Earth. But when the day comes to stand before an Awesome God, you had better be prepared.

"There is a way that seems right to a man, but its end is the way to death."
Proverbs 14:12 ESV http://bible.com/59/pro.14.12.esv

"I am speaking in human terms, because of your natural limitations. For just as you once presented your members as slaves to impurity and to lawlessness leading to more lawlessness, so now present your members as slaves to righteousness leading to sanctification. For when you were slaves of sin, you were free in regard to righteousness. But what fruit were you getting at that time from the things of which you are now ashamed? For the end of those things is death. But now that you have been set free from sin and have become slaves of God, the fruit you get leads to sanctification and its end, eternal life. For the wages of sin is death, but the free gift of God is eternal life in Christ Jesus our Lord."
Romans 6:19-23 ESV http://bible.com/59/rom.6.19-23.esv

STOP NOW!

If you know you have asked Jesus Christ to deal with the issue of sin and death in your life and you have reason to hope for Eternity in Paradise, then take a moment to praise Him and thank Him for it. You will soon be reconciled to your first love if you continue this study and follow the path clearly laid out.

If you do not know whether you have settled that matter entirely, look to the last page of this book and find a sample prayer and plan of salvation. These will lead to an opportunity to find peace, security and forgiveness.

Sexual sin attacks first at the heart of purity. Innocence is lost and the ability to see God in all His Glory begins to fade rapidly. The longing for the things of God become a contradiction to the cravings of the flesh. Even one who is a believer, once he submits to the fleshly desires of addictions like sexual gratification, loses sight of the fullness of God. Out of sight out of mind. Many addicts will say, "I have a great relationship with God, I just have this one small problem." Blinded by sin, we cannot see the sin that blinds us.

Next, addiction attacks our relationships with others. People in bondage find themselves avoiding those closest to them to keep from being found out.

In the case of sexual addiction, the addict begins to shift blame for the lack of intimacy and compassion to everyone else. "If my wife would satisfy me in bed, I would not look at those pictures." "If my wife really loved me, she would understand the magnitude of my sexual capacity." "I think my wife is frigid. She just does not like sex with me for some reason." Perhaps the real reason is the frigidity of your heart and the fact that you see sexual intimacy as something to GET and not GIVE.

Blinded by sin, we cannot see the sin that blinds us.

**SOLID ROCK
CHRISTIAN
FELLOWSHIP**

Finally, sexual sin attacks the innocents. A man who does not find it possible to constrain himself in the area of sexual passions could be lead to accomplish some of the most heinous crimes against women and children. This type of vicious attack only makes the news when it is public, or grotesque in details or magnitude. In my lifetime, there have been Bundy, Manson, Gacy, and the mechanic in Florida who had been caught and released to destroy another life. But everyday behind the closed doors of suburban homes across America, little ones have their clothes and innocence stripped away in the most subtle and devious ways.

The nature of man is so corrupt, if left to itself it will self-destruct and take as many lives with it as possible. Do not think you can decide one day to put down the magazine, turn off the internet or stop soliciting prostitutes and bath houses without Divine intervention. You may as well decide you will live to be one hundred years old and never eat another meal. Do not think you can decide one day to continue to view pornography in the little catalog in the mail and never look for something more revealing, or something real. The cycle of sexual sin is the same for every man and every woman. Re-read Romans 1: 18-32. If you started down this path, you will end on this path, unless God himself steps in to fight with you. Should you end on this path, the wake of destruction following you will only be limited by the grace of God.

Do you think a child molester just woke up one morning and said, "Wow, sex with a nine year old boy would be fun?" I think not. There is an inevitable progression. It is the downward spiral of sin which draws one further and further from reality and righteousness. It is this weakness which brings a man to utter destruction and all he holds dear vanishes like the morning dew.

As you work to clearly identify the nature, thoughts, actions and behaviors of sin in your life take some time to read the three following passages. In the space between, summarize what you've read and write down a parallel or two between the passages and your own experience.

2 Samuel 12:7-12

2 Samuel 12:13-14

1 Corinthians 6:19

LIES

There are three relationships to the lies in your life which you must manage..

1. Lies you have told.

2. Lies you have heard.

3. Lies you have believed.

Until you can identify theses lies as lies, you cannot confront them. Some of the hardest lies to identify are the lies you tell. Why do you think this is true? Unless you are intentionally manipulative, and using lies to get your own way, to control others, to plan or create circumstances and situations, the lies you tell are lies you first heard from someone else AND CHOSE TO BELIEVE.

Friends and societal norms are not trustworthy sources for truth.

Why did you choose to believe a lie? Because the liar was so persuasive? Because the truth was too painful? Because the lie makes you feel better about yourself? Because the lies are convenient or even required to maintain your sense of balance, secrecy and control?

As an addict, you may find a very blurred line between the lies you have told and the lies you have believed. Partly because of the bondage you are in, partly because your life style choices need those lies to continue. You have managed so far. If you tell and hear the same lies long enough they have become "your truth" even if they are not based in truth at all.

Some of the lies in this arena might sound like:

• "I am not a rage-aholic, I simply have a high standard for myself and others, and so few other people can meet my standards."

• "She said yes before she said no, so it wasn't really rape. Besides, I think she really liked it."

• "I am not an addict, I can choose to quit whenever I am ready."

• "That _____ is not mine. I am holding it for someone else."

• "A woman likes and needs a strong man to keep her in line."

• "Women like 'bad boys' so I am just behaving like the man she craves."

All of these are lies you have heard in society. These ideas are sold to you in books, movies, video clips, locker room conversations, even among friends and family.

Can you imagine becoming or being married to the type of person who has believed and lived out all of these lies?

The first hope to revealing and living in truth is identifying the lies which control your life choices and relationships. One way to identify a lie is to ask several people, strangers as well as friends and family, how they feel about a particular idea which to you is a strongly held belief. You will find lies to be revolting to others and yourself to be "hurt" by the reality of others disagreeing with you. If you share an idea you are passionate about and others recoil, you need to seriously consider whether you are believing a lie.

I am not suggesting you "discern or determine truth" by general consensus or by popular agreement. This is a sure fired way to find confusion. Friends and societal norms are not trustworthy sources for truth. If you determine truth based on your "circle of friends" you will find yourself in an echo chamber. Why? Because most people choose friends who believe and behave most like them. Your friends are more likely to firmly believe the same lies you do.

What about society in general? There was a time in America when slavery was a societal norm and socially acceptable, but homosexuality was not, now the opposite is acceptable. Which one is truth? Yes, it is a grotesque generalization, but it illustrates the reality that society is too fickle and ambiguous to be a source of truth.

One day everything done in darkness will be revealed. This statement has meaning on many levels. Let me address two of them here. On one level, "things done in darkness" refers to thoughts, actions, and behavior patterns which you intentionally hide from others in a planned and practiced form of deception and lies. On another level, "things done in darkness" refers to the realm of darkness, the home of wickedness and evil, these are thoughts, actions and behaviors that are rooted in the vile hatred and contempt which Satan holds for all humanity.

The first group are lies of your own choosing. Lies of convenience, lies to keep out of trouble with your wife, your boss, your pastor or maybe even legal authorities. These lies might include how often and how long you visit certain websites. These lies might include the intention of your heart when you see a lovely lady walk by. These lies might include the money you spent to feed your addiction while you were on your last business trip alone. These lies destroy relationships, betray trusts, and cover the real problem at hand.

The next group of lies are the lies imposed upon humans straight from the pit of hell. These are the lies which have told you "you will never be free of this addiction, you might as well give in." "You can't save this relationship, job, ministry, marriage, why try?" "Rape is subjective, you can't really rape your wife, she married you." "There really is no age limit to sex, those are just man made laws." (Look up NAMBLA). "Pornography is a victimless crime, like smoking weed." These lies do more than deceive the perpetrator, they destroy the hearts and souls of victims as well.

Ask yourself these five questions and write the answers here. They will be very important later in this study.

What ideas have I heard from others such as family, friends, movies, books and media which I now identify as lies?

What lies have I told to maintain control, balance or secrecy?

What lies have I believed (lies I have told or heard) which could be damaging to relationships and life style choices?

Which lies have been made up by me, lies of convenience purely for my benefit?

Which lies have been straight from the realm of darkness?

BEHAVIORS

"People do what people see." John C Maxwell

One of the best ways to identify your behaviors is to watch those you influence. If you are angry, dark and irritable, they will be too. If they lie to you, hide things from you and slither around, they likely see those things in you. It is time to take a serious inventory of the behavior which a majority of people would say defines you. As you seek this input from others be sure to inquire about what you say as well as what you do.

Begin to make note of those behaviors others point out. I mean for you to literally write them down. Good and bad behavior should be on this list. Make this list as complete and exhaustive as possible.

Next, using the list and your own judgement, make a mark next to each behavior on the list as "G" or "B." Which of these behaviors would you deem as good or bad, harmful, hurtful and potentially destructive?

Behavior, actions, things you are known for saying:

Remember to label them as to whether you think they are good or bad.

WAY OF ESCAPE

One of the greatest promises of God's Word is the promise to never leave or forsake us. Next, I believe is the promise to always leave us a "way out." You must learn to identify the way out. Is it through relationships? Is it through will power? Is it through prayer and fasting? Is it through accountability?

You need to be able to read the signs. When the darkest addictions have hold of you, you will not likely have simple strength enough to resist every temptation or opportunity. Will power alone is not enough. You are fighting against your flesh, your desires, your wants, your appetites, your cravings and simultaneously fighting a spiritual battle. Your enemy is roaming around and roaring at the back of your neck in an effort to find your weakness. When you tremble, shuffle or turn in fear he knows he's got you. Now is the time to lift your head and identify the promised way out.

Your escape may be the remote control. Turn off the TV. Your escape may be your accountability partner. Pick up the phone. Your escape may be a spiritual engagement in this skirmish. Read the Bible out loud. Pray out loud. Speak the truth from your tongue. Your escape may be in your mind alone. Change the channel inside your head, change your focus, think on things which are holy, pure and just.

I cannot over-estimate the power of changing your focus. From scripture to neuroscience, the ability God has crafted into your mind is unbelievable in its power to change your life. You can be completely transformed by renewing your mind. You can reshape your health, your relationships, your spiritual power, your eternal destiny by believing truth and acting on it, that all starts in the mind then permeates the will and emotions. When your mind, will and emotions are surrendered to the Spirit of the Living God, your body will follow suit.

There are significant studies conducted about the effect your body has on your emotional state. While posture, facial expressions, stance, arm position and eye contact will directly effect how you feel in the moment, and even effect the person you are engaged in conversation with, remember YOU MUST THINK FIRST and be intentional about behaving in a certain way before your behavior impacts your emotional state. It all starts in the mind.

CONSEQUENCES

We've got to be able to display the significance of consequences if we stand the slightest chance of making a change in the first place.

Motivation to change requires understanding there's a price to pay for every decision you make.

As an addict, you must begin to realize there's going to be a great impact on your family, on your livelihood, on your professional image, on the job you have right now for every chosen thought. If you are a ministry leader, a pastor or an executive then you have to understand the consequences of the decisions you make moment by moment as well as the legacy left by them.

Nothing changes until you do. No one changes until the pain of staying the same is greater than the pain of changing.

Consider this a swap meet. There are three significant lives you must consider and then choose from. First the life you have now, the life you will have if you stay on this path, and finally the life you desire to have, aka the life God desires for you, an abundant life. You choose one life over the other, but you only get to choose one.

The life you have now: Wherever you are in life, your friends, income, family, education, career path and your hobbies, your life is a path determined by your choices. Even the tragedies, the mistakes, the injustices which have happened "to you" afford you the power to choose how you will respond. As the popular phrases remind us; "You cannot control what happened to you, but you can control how you respond." "After any unpleasant season of your life, you can get bitter or you can get better."

The life you will have: Consider the impact of losing it all. Could you really lose your job over your addiction? Could you lose your family over your addiction? Could you lose your influence? Would you lose opportunity if your addiction was discovered but not alleviated.

The life you desire, the abundant life: Simply knowing you have the power to choose your reactions and responses increases the odds of turning life in your favor exponentially. Too many people live life as a victim and remain in bondage to their addiction simply because they want to blame someone else for their circumstances. When you take responsibility, you take back power. When you own your responses, you own the right to direct your life. When you choose thoughts, attitudes and reactions for the best life, you will live an abundant life.

Just remember, if the life is yours, the choice is yours, the benefit is yours, the power is yours, the responsibility is yours, then also, the consequences are yours. Choose wisely.

Take a few minutes right now to list three things you can see as potential or even probable consequences if your addiction is allowed to continue.

Three potential/ probable consequences:

1.

2.

3.

TRUTH

Many generations of lies are so close to truth, only more desirable. Many lies are more convenient than the truth, they tend to drown out the truth and overwhelm it.

Identifying truth is harder than it sounds. In order for us to live in truth, to act in truth, to speak the truth, we must know the truth. Lets be honest, one of the biggest challenges as an addict is the ability to hide and rationalize your problem. You might minimize and call it "a challenge." You might shift the blame and call it "someone else's fault." You might simply lie to yourself and everyone around you and say, "I don't have a problem at all, I can quit when I am ready."

Every excuse, every rationalization, every shift of blame and responsibility has the same problem, it lacks truth. You may lack an awareness of truth, you may be ignorant to the truth, you may simply deny the truth. The absence of any part of the truth is a lie. Without truth, there is no freedom! It is TRUTH who sets you free. Truth is a person and Truth is knowable. Through this journey, Truth will reveal himself to you in many ways. The facets of truth which have remained elusive, will hide from you no more. The relationship you have to truth will be transformed.

Take a moment right now and ask out loud for Truth to reveal himself to you. Call him by name, he knows his name. Ask him one specific question right now and write your answer below.

"Truth, if you love me, will you whisper to me a secret about me, which no one else knows?"

Take all the time you need. Keep reading as soon as you have written something here.

TRUTH SAID:

I know that was a weird exercise for some of you. I am confident you heard something amazing if you took the time to ask and kept asking for an answer until it came.

In the nature of your answer you might be surprised by a few things. First, the reality that Truth is not a notion, idea, political or religious rhetoric, or some divergent version of reality, but a real and living person. Second, you might be surprised by his willingness to answer your questions since your question was prefaced with, "if you love me" therefore any answer at all is a confirmation of his love for you. Finally, you may be absolutely stunned with the revelations

49

buried in his answer: He loves you. He knows you better than you know yourself, and yet he loves you. You can trust him with your deepest darkest secrets, he already knows them.

Identifying Truth is much more about learning who He is, than about learning facts and figures.

REASON TO FIGHT

Video after horrifying video, senseless fights are filmed with cell phones and shared with the world. The lack of respect for humanity, the lack of human compassion and the senseless acts of violence do not tell a good story of the condition of the human heart. The only thing worse may be the total number of views these videos are able to garner. Morbid curiosity has been elevated to a whole new level.

When I mention identifying your reason to fight, this is not what I have in mind. Rather, I imagine a mild mannered, soft spoken, fully capable grandfather who desires to hurt no one, until he must. Cross his children, hurt his grandchildren, speak ill of his wife and you will unleash a wrath the likes of which few men have ever witnessed. There are many offenses he will bear in silence. There are thousands of ways to provoke him which will be absorbed in love, grace, humility and tolerance. There is a point of no return as well. A point where life, limb and liberty are not too much to lose for the sake of Justice.

Considering all you have to lose, are you ready to lay your addiction on the other side of the scale and call it even?

Imagine the greatest rush, the most exhilarating release, the sense of euphoria in the sweet spot of your addiction. Contrast this moment with the potential consequences you listed before. Take a moment and look back at your answers in the section on consequences. If another person attempted to take from you what your addiction could, how would you respond?

List three things here you are unwilling to give up for your addiction if they were laid side by side.

1.

2.

3.

Are these consequences a price you are willing to pay, for a few moments of ecstasy?

WRONG THOUGHTS

"I once thought of love as a prison, a place I didn't want to be." This line from an old country song is a perfect example of a wrong thought.

A wrong thought is more than a thought others disagree with. A wrong thought is more than a lie. A wrong thought is an anchor or premise which allows a lie to disguise itself as a truth or principle and with which you cannot easily argue.

In the example above, love is a prison. I know very few people who want to be in prison. If I could actually make a case to demonstrate all the ways love is a prison, I could eventually convince people, love is not something you should pursue or desire. Who would want to be in love?

For decades it has been known in political circles, if you want to control the battle, control the language. Whoever wins the conversation, wins the war. Satan is willing to disguise himself as an angel of light. Satan has the audacity to lie to the face of the most powerful living being ever. Satan will whisper lies to you and then revel in your pain, anguish and demise. Every truth ever uttered has been assaulted by Satan and his minions with the intent of perverting the truth. Whatever suits his purpose to thwart the will and desire of God is fair game in Satan's mind and in his practice. Wrong thoughts are masterpieces of satanic manipulation because they are difficult to distinguish from truth. Satan is the father of lies. There is no one better at lying. There is no truth in him.

Dr. Caroline Leaf says clearly, "The mind is not something the brain does. The mind controls the brain and the brain is part of the body." This tells me the soul is in control of the ideas, feelings, emotional responses, and the physical responses brought on by addiction. While Satan may start the lies, you are responsible for believing and repeating them. The impact they have on your body can be drastic.

From a clinical perspective this may seem too simplistic but please bear with me. If the response you have to your addictive stimulus is a choice, then defeating it is as well. If what you choose to think about influences the chemical reactions in your body, then the greatest weapon against your addiction may well rest initially in the thoughts you choose to think. Wrong thoughts - wrong beliefs - wrong actions - wrong behaviors - wrong results.

If you cannot or will not classify the thoughts around you, inside you, related to your addiction as wrong and potentially harmful, you will not see them as a threat. If those thoughts are not a threat, you will not fight against them. If you will not fight against them, you will not be able to resist them or take them captive. If you do not take them captive, you cannot force them to obey.

What thoughts cross your mind on a regular basis which lead you to feel the urges of your addiction? Write at least three of them here.

Three thoughts or emotions which trigger my addictive behavior:

1.

2.

3.

RIGHT THOUGHTS

I want you to imagine driving a train through the desert sands. Fighting the resistance of the sand and gravity, battling against the directionless ambiguity of the sand at the same time. How could you steer? How could you stop? How could you get traction to begin moving in the first place?

There is a great purpose for rail road tracks! The tracks provide direction. The tracks provide traction, the tracks are a lifeline to otherwise unreachable parts of the world. Once the tracks are laid, the "way to go" is clear and manageable. Once the tracks are laid, anyone can follow them. Once the tracks are laid and the train is moving, building momentum on the tracks, it takes great effort to stop a train without the cooperation of the train.

Why do you think we use the phrase "train of thought"? When your mind is "on the track" building momentum, it is hard to stop. Has anyone ever accused you of having a "one track mind"? This is a sign of your addiction. Have you ever seen a dog who loves to play with a ball or toy and is so obsessive about his toy, he would literally run into traffic to retrieve it?

This illustrates the power of right thinking. Choosing the right thoughts is a simple start, but a beginning which will determine or undermine your long term success.

Once you have locked in on a train of thought, of the right thoughts, you can redirect anything in your life from health, to wealth to relationships and yes even power over your addiction. So by now you might be wondering, if these "right thoughts" can be so life changing, where do I find them? How do I know what thoughts are right and how do I implement this "thinking strategy"?

For a list of "right thoughts" take a moment right now to read Philippians 4:8-12. Studying these few verses, write a list below of five "right thoughts" which you feel are new and contradictory to the thoughts which surround your addiction.

Right thoughts contrary to the thoughts of my addiction:

1.

2.

3.

4.

5.

WHO YOU HURT

If you have never considered the pain of the silent victims of sexual assault, pornography, drug abuse, alcoholism, sex trafficking, workaholism, or narcissism, you have no idea how deep the pain might be buried. If someone you know personally and care for deeply is carrying the burden of being a victim in the past, the unspoken torture they endure at your hand is hard to fathom. Perhaps they say nothing when you treat them like an object. Perhaps they blame themselves for they words you say to them. Perhaps they justify the silent manipulation in your relationship as self-protection. Chances are, you as an addict, have not even noticed how your choices in thought, word and deed have crushed their soul. If you had asked me in the height of my addiction which ways I abuse my wife, I could have recognized none. Does my lack of recognizing her pain eliminate or minimize it?

Victim's Letters
From the many who have suffered this addiction, it takes being accountable to a Christian mentor. I would highly encourage you to join a men's accountability group.

My ex husband had strong addiction to pornography and it destroyed our marriage. He did not see me for who I was, but as an object of his sexual fantasy of other women. Unfortunately, many who are addicted to porn, see women as objects, and we who are on the other end of the addiction feel "used", we feel like an "object" to them. It also leads to marital rape and many men who have been involved in pornography admit losing control during love making with their wives because their minds are not with their wives during this time but with other women they are fantasizing about during intercourse. They are so involved in their love making in their wish for another woman, they forget who they are with and they do not hear the words stop or cries for them to stop. It becomes an act of aggression and anger at his wife during the love making because he holds the image of the other woman in mind.

Please, Please, I beg you before you lose any female relationship you may have or could have, get the help and healing you need before this ever happens to the one you truly love.

I have healed a lot from the marital rape and I can now talk without shutting down. I want you to hear me. You have made the first step by coming out of the darkness. The second step is to step on your pride and talk to someone who is close to you. A good accountability partner who could lead you out of this sexual sin and help you grow deeper into your walk with God. If there is a possibility of a men's group therapy, it was suggested to my now ex-husband to become involved in group therapy.

I believe this would help you as it has helped me to become involved in sexual abuse support groups so God could bring healing to me and to help me to be able to forgive the perpetrators.

If you are near the Dallas area, I encourage you to look up this

program and could find much healing in this - look this up:
www.theroadadventure.org These are seminars led by volunteers
who have gone through similar things and have found healing.
There is hope and there is healing.
May God richly bless you today and always,
Posted on 4/11 6:21 AM | IP: 64.48.234.27

Please pray that I break away from the sin of pornography. I have
struggled with this for so long and I don't know how to get out of
it. I'm in a ministry position and cannot live this life of hypocrisy
anymore. If those I work with found out about this, my ministry
would be gone. I am taking steps to get away from it, but it seems
like my willpower dies when I am online.

God forgive me for the sin I have engaged in, in your eyes. Please
don't take your love away from me and my family for what I'm
doing. Help me break free so I can enjoy true intimacy with my
wife and not pictures and videos on a screen. I don't want to feel
like this anymore.

Wash me white, O God. Make me reborn, as your Son is reborn.
Help me live in Him and not in sin.

Amen
Posted on 4/10 10:56 PM

If you think you can carry on in this sin and no one will be
affected, you are a fool. You have already hurt more people than
you know. If you encouraged your son to participate in the leering
looks, or allowed you daughter to observe it, they have been
impacted. If you have imagined another lover while with your
mate, your mate has been impacted. If you have made demands of
time, or behavior which violated the conscience of your mate,

60

they have been impacted. If you think your masturbation or pornography are a personal thing and have no bearing on the people in your life, think again. Just ask your wife how your jealousy and coldness breaks her heart. Just ask your daughter how the separation and isolation has left her looking for love from anywhere and how the "affection" you modeled before her has shaped her aspirations of being a good woman when she is older. Just ask your son if he has found your stash or web history and what he thought of it.

Ask yourself these questions:

1. "If my wife had the same images in her head of other men and fantasized about them when she was with me, what spectrum of emotion would flood over me?"

2. "If I knew another man exposed my children to the same stuff I hide from them, what would I do about it?"

3. "If I replaced my wife with any of my fantasy lovers, would any of them love me like she does now?" "Would they still love me twenty years from now?"

Do you still think that sexual sin is a private and victimless sin?

How then shall we live? We need help and direction. We need encouragement and discipline. We need grace and mercy and patience. We need Jesus and we need forgiveness.

SUMMARY & ACTION

When David looked on Bathsheba's form, he thought...

His thoughts lead to an impulse to act...

His actions lead to an adulterous, sinful, affair and the premeditated murder of her husband...

When cornered by the prophet, David still did not identify his sin as sin until the illustration was given. Even in the illustration, David's own sense of justice and righteousness raged against the bad actions in the story until the prophet told him, "David, you are that man."

In an instant, awareness of his error, sin, destruction and harm to others overwhelmed him. David tore his clothes and cried out to God in repentance and asked for God's forgiveness. While his sin was forgiven and his right relationship to God restored, David still endured horrific consequences for his choices and it all started with a thought.

Read James 1:13-15 and write out the stages of sin which leads to death.

Read the story of David and Bathsheba and list at least one of the severe consequences David endured for his sin.

1.

CONFESS

Confession is realizing and admitting, what God said all along is true and you believe it.

SIN

90% of the people in Hell will be there for one reason: because they refused to change. Changing means first admitting that you were wrong. Sin is any thought or behavior in you, not desired by God.

Confess

a. To God to be forgiven

b. To friends to be prayed for

c. To those you have hurt to be reconciled (see section Those You Have Hurt)

Sexual sin is "natural" (flesh). Being obedient to our "natural" desires rather than to God (spirit) is sin. Now, let's address what to do about sin and move on with your life of spiritual growth.

In my experience there are four basic but mandatory steps to freedom and recovery of any kind.

1. Identify the sin – what specifically about my behavior, thoughts or words is contrary to scripture?

2. Confess the sin – speak God's word over your thoughts and actions

3. Repent of the sin – Change your mind about your sin nature and align your thoughts with God's thoughts so that sin is no longer your natural reaction to temptation.

4. Forgiveness - ask God to forgive you for your sin and live constantly forgiving others as quickly as possible.

If these steps looks familiar it should. This book is a detailed application of this simplified process. The power in these four steps transcends time, culture, age and the nature of sin itself. These steps have the ability to restore a right relationship to God through Jesus Christ without regard for the type of sin you are in bondage to, the length of time you have been in bondage or how acceptable your sin of choice is in your culture.

For example, the abuse of a spouse through over-bearing verbal commands, or subservient treatment is culturally acceptable in many nations, but it is a violation of the principles of a godly relationship as defined by holy scripture. Perhaps your family has exhibited this tradition for 20 generations, and it is acceptable to them. It does not change this fact; it breaks the heart of God, who created men and women to be a reflection of the relationship between Christ and the Church, His bride. Christ loved her so much he laid down his life for her. Men are to love their brides the same way, devotedly, sacrificially and always putting her needs first.

In the last chapter we talked about the sin of addiction itself, how it attacks from nowhere or so it seems. You know it can control every waking moment to the point of obsession. You know by now there are victims of your addicted behavior when it controls you and they are usually those you love the most.

When you have enough conviction to look at this issue in your life and say, "Yep, that's sin." You have accomplished step one, which believe it or not is the hardest part. You could go on in denial forever, not recognizing, or acknowledging your sin. In fact you might even carry on for years loving the behavior you have become accustomed to and not revel in the idea of giving it up. If that is you, ouch, you are in for a lot of pain. God will do whatever it takes to humble you, to break your heart, to bring you to the place where you weep for your sin and the pain it has caused. When he does, you will long for the hope to walk away free. You will cry out to God from a broken and contrite heart, filled with shame, guilt and grief. God will hear you and he will come to your rescue.

Then you, like David, will be forced to see your sin for what it is. Here is David's confession.

> "Have mercy on me, O God, according to your steadfast love; according to your abundant mercy blot out my transgressions. Wash me thoroughly from my iniquity, and cleanse me from my sin! For I know my transgressions, and my sin is ever before me. Against you, you only, have I

sinned and done what is evil in your sight, so that you may be justified in your words and blameless in your judgment. Behold, I was brought forth in iniquity, and in sin did my mother conceive me. Behold, you delight in truth in the inward being, and you teach me wisdom in the secret heart. Purge me with hyssop, and I shall be clean; wash me, and I shall be whiter than snow. Let me hear joy and gladness; let the bones that you have broken rejoice. Hide your face from my sins, and blot out all my iniquities. Create in me a clean heart, O God, and renew a right spirit within me. Cast me not away from your presence, and take not your Holy Spirit from me. Restore to me the joy of your salvation, and uphold me with a willing spirit. Then I will teach transgressors your ways, and sinners will return to you. Deliver me from bloodguiltiness, O God, O God of my salvation, and my tongue will sing aloud of your righteousness. O Lord, open my lips, and my mouth will declare your praise. For you will not delight in sacrifice, or I would give it; you will not be pleased with a burnt offering. The sacrifices of God are a broken spirit; a broken and contrite heart, O God, you will not despise."
Psalms 51:1-17 ESV http://bible.com/59/psa.51.1-17.esv

The point is this. God knows you better than you know yourself. He also loves you more than you love yourself. He knows what sin binds you, what damage it has done and is still doing. Confession of sin is no trick. It is not some magical way to get God and others to sympathize with your pain and misery. It is not a tool to force God to forgive you. Confession of sin is more like a trip to the dentist. You know your rotten tooth is causing you pain, you know carrying on without doing something about it will only cause more pain. You know the dentist is the pro when it comes to toothaches and cavities. If you want to get an end to this pain, you must go see the dentist, tell him where it hurts and then let him go to work to do what needs to be done. If you sat around on your couch in pain for a week or so and did not tell the dentist what the problem was, what are the chances the pain would go away? Slim? None? Why would we want to do that? Perhaps out of fear of the dentist. Perhaps we are ashamed to reveal we have a cavity. Perhaps we cannot afford the trip to the dentist. Maybe we just love cavities!

When it comes to sin, all of these excuses are without merit. We need not fear a God who loves each of his children so much. We need not be ashamed in His presence because he longs for us and loved us first, even while we were yet sinners. The price for sin is high to be sure, but it has already been paid for. The cross has no co-pay and no deductible.

> ""Come now, let us reason together, says the Lord: though your sins are like scarlet, they shall be as white as snow; though they are red like crimson, they shall become like wool." Isaiah 1:18 ESV http://bible.com/59/isa.1.18.esv

Confession is not commiserating. Confession is not gossiping. Confession is not begging. Confession is realizing and admitting what God said all along is true, and you believe it. Confession is asking God to do what is necessary to eradicate the pain. Pull it, crown it, cap it, do a root canal. Anything but ignore it.

71

Confession is admitting you were wrong and asking for help to change. Confession is the second step on the long and hard road to freedom and recovery. Confession to God allows the merciful heart of God to offer forgiveness and for you to accept it.

Confession among believers: I am a strong advocate of accountability, but not as many understand accountability. Many have this picture of accountability as a meeting man to man or group of men sitting around and "confessing" to one another in what ways they have failed or sinned since they last met together. I honestly see no benefit to such commiserating. In my opinion, it lends to three undesirable affects.

Comparison: Many men will hear the nature of sin in another person's life and say to himself, "Well, I am not as bad as him so why am I even here?" He might even become haughty in spirit as a result because he is comparing himself to a brother who is fallen rather than to Christ who is meant to be our example and our judge.

Lasciviousness: Some men will become curious about the behavioral habits of the others with whom they "share". This can lead to becoming hardened at heart to the sin they carry themselves and an allowance or license to continue in sin, perpetuating the problem rather than confronting it.

Judgment. The inequity between those who meet as to their place in the journey, spiritual maturity, psychological maturity and status or position in the body of Christ can cause one person to share and become vulnerable where the other person is somewhat sheltered from the same vulnerability. This inequity can cause judgmental attitudes, fear and shame, which again increase the difficulties with isolation and avoidance rather than confronting them.

Rather, I feel confession of sin to your brother should be two-fold. First, it should be in courage and boldness declaring war against your sin. Acknowledging the battles you fight gives room for others to join in the fight. Secondly, it should be done in the confidence that you will be directed by a mature believer to face the sin, deal with it, repent of it and pursue Christ instead.

> "Therefore, confess your sins to one another and pray for one another, that you may be healed. The prayer of a righteous person has great power as it is working."
> James 5:16 ESV http://bible.com/59/jas.5.16.esv.

In a godly accountability relationship, a confession might include how one has looked, stared and fantasized about those around him or those of the past. It must also include thoughts which you identified as sins of the addiction before they became sinful action. This is one of the most powerful parts of confession for two reasons. First, confession of the invisible but potent thoughts in your mind reinforces the identification of those damaging thoughts, sharpens your awareness of similar thoughts, and prepares you to take every thought captive which lifts itself up against the knowledge of God. Second, this type of confession is a declaration for the kingdom of darkness, giving notice you are on the lookout, actively guarding against corrupt thoughts which can destroy the soul. If you resist the devil, he will flee. If you do not resist the devil, he will enslave you.

> "Submit yourselves therefore to God. Resist the devil, and he will flee from you. Draw near to God, and he will draw near to you. Cleanse your hands, you sinners, and purify your hearts, you double-minded. Be wretched and mourn and weep. Let your laughter be turned to mourning and your joy to gloom. Humble yourselves before the Lord, and he will exalt you."
> James 4:7-10 ESV http://bible.com/59/jas.4.7-10.esv

Your accountability partner, or mentor, should encourage you to seek God in prayer for strength, pray with you and for you for a change of heart and a new passion, then direct you to place in scripture which would give more insight and strength for avoiding and resisting temptation. Additionally, a godly mentor should look for opportunities to encounter you on a regular basis whether face to face or on the phone, to remind you that you are being prayed for, offer Biblical suggestions for pursuing freedom, and practical solutions from their own victorious experiences.

"I found that to avoid staring and entertaining sexual thoughts about an attractive woman, all I have to remember is Proverbs 26:11. When I think about a dog licking up his own vomit, I am turned off by the idea that I am a fool returning to my folly and doing things I hate about me. Maybe you should try that." Loren

LIES

As the body of her husband was being dragged away, the dust had not settled from the marks left by his feet and yet Sapphira continued the conspiratorial deception, and she paid the same price. Pause now and read Acts 5:1-10.

Sometimes the hardest part of confessing lies rests in the reality, you have already told so many lies, to so many people, in so many ways, it's hard to remember which lie to confess to whom and why.

Can you imagine trying to straighten into a single strand a spiders web? Detaching the crossing strands, unwinding the circular logic, dismantling the architecture which stands against the storm would be a daunting task. It would be the same task to try to untangle the many lies you have told to hide and protect your addiction.

In "Identify: Lies", you were asked to list some lies you have believed and told. Now is the time to begin your untangling. This untangling will be a three step process.

1. Speak specifically the lies you have believed and repeated. Write them here.

2. Voice to yourself and to God what it is about this lie which makes it a lie. What makes it not true? Write it here.

3. Speak out loud the truth which counters this lie. Write it here.

This is a key step to your freedom. Do not underestimate the power of confessing the lies which have dominated and controlled your life. When you can replace the lies and speak truth in their place, you will be empowered in a new way. Use a separate page to continue this list if need be. Then place that extra page as a book mark in this chapter.

BEHAVIORS

Who broke my favorite coffee cup?!?

As you look at the toddler with coffee stains on their shirt, you realize the answer is obvious but still no admission or confession is forthcoming. All you want is an "I'm sorry daddy." All you get is a puzzled look and a shrug of the shoulders. No one apparently, broke your cup.

In the last section we identified the behaviors which are sinful, destructive and harmful. Now we must be willing to confess to our part in those behaviors. Taking responsibility is a major part of maturity. In life and in the Christian faith, those who cannot or will not take responsibility for their actions and the consequences caused by them, will remain unable to grow in any other area.

The act of confession in this arena is both powerful and profound. Remember, this is not groveling and complaining about your current circumstance, this confession is not a request for reprieve from your consequences, it is primarily a verbalized agreement with God about the facts.

You will need to look back on your list in "Identify: Behaviors" to complete this step. As you look over this list, read it out loud. Take some time to pray and ask The Holy Spirit what his opinion is of each behavior.

Look back on your judgement of good and bad, and focus your mind on God's answer compared to yours. Your confession is complete when you agree. Read Isaiah 1:18 for a deeper understanding of this process. We will discuss alignment in greater detail when we get to repentance.

Using the remainder of this page, list and then read aloud, the specific behaviors which have brought pain, shame and guilt to those you love most and to God himself.

WAY OF ESCAPE

An ounce of prevention is worth a pound of cure. Awareness is an extremely powerful tool for healing, defense and protection.

You must be willing to proclaim, declare and confess the efforts of God on your behalf. This exercise will increase your faith, express your gratitude to him and send the forces of temptation away with their tails between their legs. God's promise to his children is multifaceted. One crucial aspect includes a promised "way of escape" or way out of sin.

The ability of God to see you when you are trapped and tempted is an aspect of his omniscience. The desire for him to protect you from temptation is an aspect of his incredible love for you. The power of God to throw you a lifeline in any circumstance is an expression of his commitment to your well-being and abundant life.

For the next 90 days, I want you to keep record of every time you are tempted to surrender like a slave to your addiction. I want you to write the way of escape the Father offers you as well. Then I want you to take a moment to say Thank You Father for this way of escape.

1. Acknowledge the moment of temptation in writing and aloud.

2. Acknowledge the specific way of escape in writing and aloud.

3. Acknowledge how frequently you experience the same source or path of temptation and how often the way of escape is the same. Do this in writing so you can look back on it for years and mentor others to healing and freedom. Do this aloud so you can give thanks to God and notice to the enemy of your soul.

CONSEQUENCES

Whatever you plant will grow. If you don't plant it, don't expect it to grow. If you plant jalapeños, don't expect to harvest cherries.

You will not escape the consequences of your sin. Your addiction has a price like every other choice. Some will pay the price in the loss of a job. Some will pay the price in the loss of their family, wealth, possessions or influence. Nonetheless, a price must be paid for what you have done and the lives you have impacted.

As mentioned earlier, a significant sign of maturity is found in the ability to accept blame and to take responsibility for your actions. While this section might appear to be very brief, the response it requires of you will be quite demanding.

Take some time (about 20 minutes) to reflect on the behavior you have marked as bad and agreed with God to be bad as well. It's time to measure the behavior against potential consequences and verbalize your acceptance of the consequences.

Some consequences will remain unknown to you until a later time. Some will be immediate and obvious. Some will be beyond your control such as legal ramifications, a spouse's choice to end your marriage, a loss of privilege and authority or certain fines. List as many consequences as you can realistically imagine being associated with your addiction and resulting behavior, it is very important for you to verbalize and record them in writing.

BEHAVIOR   **POTENTIAL CONSEQUENCE**

TRUTH

Speak life. Jesus said, "I am the way, the truth and the life."

Knowing truth will set you free. He is powerful beyond your imagination. He chose to lay down his life and he chose to take it up again. He chose!! When you agree with God's word about anything, you are the one transformed.

Have you ever noticed the impact a significant revelation has when you speak it aloud? There really is something different from just thinking through the revelation. Verbal confession is a weapon and this is a place to battle with full force and passion.

Jesus was not puzzled about Peter's understanding of who he was. Jesus knows your every thought and Peter's thoughts as well. When Jesus asked the disciples, who do men say that I am, they had many answers. When Jesus asked Peter the same question, Peter had one brief, profound answer. In response to Peter's answer, Jesus confirmed the answer and affirmed his friend by saying, "This revelation was not given to you by man, but by the power of the Holy Spirit and upon this revelation, I will build my church." I believe Peter had the answer deep in his heart, deep in his soul embedded there by the Spirit of God. I also believe there is a real possibility Peter had not completed the thought nor experienced the significance of the revelation until he answered Jesus' question.

So let me ask who? Who do you say Jesus is? Write your answer here to complete and organize your thoughts and then read your answer aloud several times. The KING is listening, He will respond.

REASON TO FIGHT

If you have ever witnessed a fight as it begins to gain momentum you know the nature of intimidation.

There are times when the mere tone or volume of your voice will end a fight before the first blow. In fact, in karate, one of the first lessons is assuming a firm fighting stance combined with a very loud "kiaa." It is taught to create an awareness. Many people want to intimidate you more than they want to fight you.

Now is the time for you to verbalize, aloud, and with passionate authority just how determined you are to win this war raging within.

You have listed and expressed your wrong choices and your wrong doing.

You have recounted where you went wrong in the battle and spoken aloud the many ways God offered, and will continue to offer for you to escape the bondage of your addiction.

You have pondered and verbalized everything you stand to lose.

You have decided to keep what God has given you and make no room for sin.

Now is the time to declare your willingness and preparedness to fight! Let God know, (he already knows) just how badly you want to live an abundant life in righteousness. Let the enemy know how determined you are to sacrifice yourself for the sake of everything you stand to lose.

This exercise is the equivalent of sharpening your sword before battle, but doing it where your enemy cannot avoid watching.

Again, organize your thoughts and record them here, then read them aloud several times. Loudly declare your confession of faith and preparedness for battle. If you resist the devil, he will flee from you.

WRONG THOUGHTS

Now is the time to unwind the spider web. You will need to apply your thinking cap and some diligent, committed time. Over the course of your life and addiction you have undoubtedly lived and acted with some distorted views and beliefs.

These views have lead you to see life, thoughts and people through specific lenses. An example "wrong thought lens" would be racism, sexism or any other prejudice based on created characteristics of another person.

Another specific example might be the expectations placed on your spouse. Perhaps it starts with a phrase like, "Women should...", "A good wife would...", "If you really loved me..." All of these are wrong thoughts which lead to poor communications at best and abuse if not identified and corrected.

Your distorted beliefs might have caused you to trust people you should not, distrust people you should trust and judge others without relationship.

Take a moment and reflect on some of the wrong thoughts which have guided your choices in people and perceptions. Once again, I want you to write out the specific thoughts which have lead you down a dangerous path.

You will need to do this exercise more than once as you identify other additional wrong thoughts in your communications and relationships.

1. Write out how the thought was formulated or created in your thinking. Did you hear it growing up? Was this notion or thought created in response to your own painful experiences?

2. Write out the people and relationships which have been impacted by these thoughts. Who have you hurt as you expressed these ideas verbally or in action and treatment?

3. Write out the correction to this idea or thought. What does God say about this way of thinking or treating people?

4. Speak these confessions aloud to gain power over them.

RIGHT THOUGHTS

Confession is one of the most powerful tools in the universe. In fact, there are people who believe their right to speak anything they wish will cause the universe to obey their thoughts and words.

While I do not fully agree with the worldview developed around this practice, I can say with confidence, you were created in the image of God and He spoke the very universe into existence. With His voice he stopped the Devil, split the Red Sea in half, spoke to the raging storm to silence it, raised Lazarus from the dead, cast out devils and empowered the saints to do the same. When we agree with His agenda, His directions, His purpose, His Word and speak to the universe He created… the universe must obey Him.

Confession of right thoughts is a practice of speaking aloud what God has already spoken over you, in you and through you. It is a practice which requires reading and understanding His Word so you can agree and apply what He said.

Looking back to page 55 of this book, take a few minutes to speak aloud what you wrote in the five spaces. You should repeat these thoughts again and again until they become part of your everyday language and way of thinking.

Repeating them aloud will begin this process of creating new neuro-pathways inside your brain. After you have practiced with the list in "Identify: Right Thoughts," begin to make a new list here. Again, write them out, then read them aloud several times.

Right thoughts I want to guide my life choices and actions:

From "Identify: Right Thoughts"

1.

2.

3.

4.

5.

New thoughts

1.

2.

3.

4.

5.

WHO YOU HURT

CONFESS TO THOSE YOU HAVE HURT

This is by far the most controversial issue within the recovery from sexual addiction. Before I present my opinion, let me say, some of the best professionals disagree on this issue and the odds everyone will agree with me are slim. For that reason, I suggest you personally seek God for each individual and each instance, then listen very closely for HIS guidance before you decide which course of action suits your particular set of circumstances.

"There are some things better left unsaid" certainly applies to sexual sin. Some would say a pure and honest relationship with your spouse or spouse to be, requires you to "come clean" about everything you have done in your life in this arena. They would also say, failure to do so is tantamount to lying and cheating. I did this. Before I married my wife, she knew everything I had done, with whom and how old I was when it happened. Was this wise? I cannot tell you. I can look back now, married since 1994 and say beyond question, my wife has an immeasurable gift of grace. She accepted me even with all this knowledge. She accepted who I was and our life has been greatly blessed because of the foundation of transparency and honesty. Don't get me wrong. It has not come without some pain, shame and guilt. Only time has removed concerns and suspicions about how much of my life was still given over to sin. There have been seasons of relapse when the very nature of our intimate relationship was under fire from my unrealistic expectations and desires. But all in all, it has proven to be the right thing for me to be completely honest with my wife about everything.

In my past I have hurt many people by engaging in inappropriate activities with them. Many of them, I have had opportunity to visit with and share my new life in Christ. I asked for them to forgive me for the pain I caused them and the sin to which I exposed them.   Again, this must be considered with measured caution and spiritual guidance.

It is altogether possible, total honesty and transparency could open old wounds almost healed, or cause suspicions and concerns created by misunderstanding or misinterpretation. This can cause a lot of unnecessary pain for many people which can become beyond repair very quickly.

I know men who have revealed to their wife a struggle with pornography and masturbation only to find the shame and jealousy it stirs up results in her leaving or refusing to be intimate any longer. Pray a lot, seek godly counsel and consider the circumstance before you say anything. There may be things and relationships that are better left alone and confessed only to God. Seek counseling with a godly, Biblically-based counselor to gain better understanding, then invite your spouse only if your counselor's professional opinion advises it.

I heard one professional therapist tell a client his burden of guilt, while heavy and destructive, did not warrant sharing with his spouse. The concept was, if the issue had been eradicated and measures had been taken to ensure it would not happen again, there was no good to come of hurting his wife with the details of a long since past affair.

I am afraid that advice on this issue is as varied as the individual circumstances and personalities involved. Some will handle such a revelation better than others. Some will cry and pray and lend strength and scrutiny to be an over-comer, others will be crushed and will flee. Be careful and thoughtful and ask yourself if this confession is for your sake (to relieve guilt) or the sake of others.

Bottom line, you must confess to God to be forgiven. You must confess to your brothers to be prayed for. You must consider whether your confession to your victims is for your good or theirs and proceed with godly wisdom and caution.

SUMMARY & ACTION

It is my hope and intention for you to experience the power of confession to genuinely change every aspect of your life as you move through this process.

Confession is not begging for forgiveness. Confession is not groveling in misery and guilt. Confession is not declaring to the universe ideas of your own making. Confession is not some manipulation of a relationship designed to relieve your guilt or prevent consequences.

Confession is agreeing with God, through His written word and prayer, about your thoughts, your behavior, your choices and your spiritual position. Confession is a tool for reminding your soul and the enemy of your soul, Christ has the final word! When Jesus says you are forgiven, YOU ARE FORGIVEN! No one, nothing, no power on earth or in Hell can change the reality of redemption.

Confession has the power to transform your thinking and bring it into alignment with truth.

Writing your conclusions and confessions is a practice designed to both leave the legacy of your learning and a mark on the door post to remind you just how much you have grown, conquered and overcome.

Failure to write out what you confess aloud, could offer the enemy a chance to debate whether you have covered this ground before now. Have you fought this battle before and won? Have you never faced this battle? These questions will come up, journaling will be your evidence. Do not skip this step in confession.

Speaking with your voice demands conviction and passion. You will need to be convinced of the words for them to be spoken with authority. You will need to be passionate about the battle itself in order to speak at all. Your silence in the moment of confession will be deafening. Your willingness to give ground without rebuttal will invite the enemy to claim more ground.

REPENT

One of the most controversial terms in Christianity , repent, means simply to think differently.

SIN

Sin is "natural" but we should not be. Walk after the Spirit and you will not fulfill the lusts of the flesh.

You can take away the power of the enemy by changing the way you think about sin and choices. I believe this is true repentance.

Slavery versus ownership, temptation versus self control, submission to sin versus submission to the spirit of God, choice is the key to the power of holiness.

Compare Galatians 5:22 with 2 Peter 1:5-8 and you will see that the fruit of the spirit is a gift from God, but there are certain aspects we must make effort to incorporate ourselves. Then look at 2 Peter 1:3-9, God has given us divine power for life and godliness.

In my selfishness and pride, I believed that my desire, my cravings and my satisfaction were first and foremost, the most important thing at any moment in time. Not my wife, not my children, not my God, just my addiction. I did what came naturally with no regard for the consequences. I was proud enough to believe I deserved to be treated to this pleasure. I was convinced that my urges were my directions and that my body should determine the outcome.

Self-control was a shadow of a thought, even good sense was often abandoned. Doing in my imagination what I thought I could never do in real life. Then eventually doing in real life what I thought I would have never even imagined. I was a slave to sin. It beckoned and I came running. It owned me, and I allowed it.

You must choose to stop doing those things that have been the patterns and habits of your life for so long. Those activities that represent the sin that binds you are obvious. Masturbation, pornography, sexual immorality, drug use, abuse of alcohol, control or rage, or any other sexual sins these are all sins of choice.

I know of no time in my twenty plus years of struggle, when self-stimulation happened TO me without my willingness to participate. I can think of no time when my computer woke me up in the middle of the night, pulled back the covers and flashed nude pictures in my face. I don't recall ever meeting someone who was stalked by illicit drugs, crack pipes or liquor bottles. If these things happened in my life or yours it was because I sought them out and so did you! I craved them and gave in to them and they consumed me like a fire.

Yes, these urges for pleasure and relaxation are natural. Yes, the need for sexual intimacy is a God given gift. About now you might be thinking that God did this to you. He gave you the desire and the ability to satisfy it. He did. He also told you clearly the proper use and place for your desire. He also told you the proper context and acceptable behavior to meet those cravings. But what He did NOT do was tempt you to sin. What He did NOT do was cause you to lust outside of His will or cause you or to crave what was not yours to have. You chose to do that, all on your own.

> James 1:12 Blessed is the man that endureth temptation; for when he hath been approved, he shall receive the crown of life, which the Lord promised to them that love him. Let no man say when he is tempted, I am tempted of God; for God cannot be tempted with evil, and he himself tempteth no man: but each man is tempted, when he is drawn away by his own lust, and enticed. Then the lust, when it hath conceived, beareth sin: and the sin, when it is fullgrown, bringeth forth death. Be not deceived, my beloved brethren. Every good gift and every perfect gift is from above, coming down from the Father of lights, with whom can be no variation, neither shadow that is cast by turning.

First, we lust. Then, we are enticed. When we give in to lust it bears a child named sin. When sin is full grown, it is called death. If you want to live, you must choose life. You must choose to resist the temptation of lust, alcohol, drugs or whatever draws you to think and behave in a way contrary to God's thoughts. You must choose not to wet yourself when the urge comes over you. <u>God will not do this for you</u>. It is your choice. It requires your will. It demands your attention. Your thoughts will not change on their own accord. You must take every thought captive.

Resist. Flee. Walk away. Then cry out for help...

When we discuss the finality of death, we often leave out the best part. There is another side. There is a side beyond death. That too is your choice: death in sin or death to sin.

"Dead Men Don't Wear Plaid" was a really bad movie in the early eighties. I never saw the movie but the title intrigued me. If dead men don't wear plaid, what else don't they do? Well they don't cough. They don't sneeze. They don't laugh. They also don't masturbate. Dead men don't smoke or drink or chew or go out with girls who do.

> Mark 8:33 ...Get thee behind me, Satan; for thou mindest not the things of God, but the things of men. And he called unto him the multitude with his disciples, and said unto them, If any man would come after me, <u>let him deny himself</u>, and take up his cross, and follow me. For whosoever would save his life shall lose it; and whosoever shall lose his life for my sake and the gospel's shall save it. For what doth it profit a man, to gain the whole world, and forfeit his life? For what should a man give in exchange for his life? For whosoever shall be ashamed of me and of my words in this adulterous and sinful generation, the Son of man also shall be ashamed of him, when he cometh in the glory of his Father with the holy angels.

W. Tozer noted wisely, the man who went to the cross never came back. He had said his farewells. The man who takes up his cross to follow Jesus should be under no false assumptions one-day things will be back to normal. If you have been, you are mistaken. There is not a place for prayer and pornography to peacefully coexist. There is no place for fasting with prostitutes in the temple.

There is no room on this journey for looking back and longing for what was before. Remember the sin of the Israelites who died in the dessert was their lack of faith. What God had in store for them was better than their craving for the things of the flesh they had left behind in Egypt. They did not believe. They did not agree with God's thoughts.

He sent the spies back with the tales of a land of great glory and wonderful fruits. But only two of the twelve spies really got it, and only they GOT IT. The others died after 40 years of nothingness and wandering in the hot sands of the dessert. They marched the same march, craved the same fleshpots and melons until they all died off. Only the few who chose to believe God would keep His promise to fulfill them and meet their every need actually saw the glorious treasures which awaited them in Canaan. (Read Numbers 13-14)

If you are asking yourself what this has to do with God's part in overcoming this sin, just sit tight. It is about to knock you out of your chair.

Your ability to believe your addiction is the only means to true satisfaction; your willingness to give yourself to a harlot and the wiles of pornography, to the control of a substance indicates you have not yet grasped what awaits you on the other side. You have been deceived by the best. You are convinced like Eve, that you have been lied to.

**SOLID ROCK
CHRISTIAN
FELLOWSHIP**

You know in your feeble little mind God does not really want you to have it all. He is holding one hand behind His back and keeping from you what you really want. He is cheating you. Right?

God promised to give you a desire for the wife of your youth. He promised if you made her the object of your grandest affection and Him the desire of your heart, everything you ever longed for would pale in comparison. What fools must we be to trade a melon for a land flowing with milk and honey? What fools must we be to trade hours before the computer or video screen or magazine for the intimate embrace of a wife who longs for nothing more than an opportunity to leave us in the rapturous atmosphere of an unforgettable sexual encounter? What fools must we be to trade the desires of the flesh for eternity with a loving and almighty God?

What is God's part?

Put away the "childish things" and get your face in His WORD, that is the only place to find it! You will find more than you ever thought to ask for awaiting you in a place you never thought to go.

Don't Look Back ~ by James L. Norris ~ 30 November 1991

Sirens screamed in the background, as they ran from the building. The structure wasn't quite as sound as we once thought. Each step was more questionable. Every second was more frightening. The heat was intense and there seemed to be no escape. I looked on from outside. I saw the roof collapse and the stairway suddenly became part of the ground floor. I began to shake with fear for the men trying to rescue those still trapped inside.

I heard someone yell, "That's the last victim. Get everyone out before she goes!" My heart raced with joy. What a success. I saw the last firefighter running for the door. He had all his equipment but otherwise he was empty handed. The wall of flames appeared to be chasing him. He ran with all he had. Looking over his shoulder every-other step, he tried desperately to out run the fire. The chief yelled out "Don't look back! Keep your stride, you're gonna be all right!"

He glanced back as he cleared the last interior wall. His feet got tangled in the masses of debris on the floor. He began to stumble. Falling forward, his momentum was at least enough to get him to the door. Just before he fell, someone came as if from nowhere. Rushing into the picture from far right he tackled the falling man. The momentum of both carried them both far enough to be safe. One more second and he would have been a dead man. The fall nearly took his life. The love of a stranger saved it!

When we go through life, so often we keep looking back on our mistakes. We can't seem to look ahead. Ironically, we won't see where we are going if we keep looking back.

The Cross was like the doorway in the previous story. It was our last threshold. It was not just the stopping point for the torment and torture that pursued us; it was the opening and the rescue; the starting point; another chance to live. We should keep our eyes forward. "Seek ye first the Kingdom of God..." Remember our past was all about the world, Satan, and discontent.

Don't look back! The Devil is behind you!

LIES

BONDAGE

Many men have faced the challenge of sexual addiction and walked away with no hope of conquering the beast. It seems to me the issue of addiction itself has morphed into more than it really was.

Have you ever been bitten by a toothless dog?

Have you ever been beaten with a wet noodle?

Have you even been slashed with a sponge or stabbed with a napkin?

I know as you are reading this book you are asking yourself if I have any clue what you are struggling against. Let me answer with a resounding YES!! I became sexually active at nine years old. I wrestled with the uncontrollable bondage and raging desires for twenty-five years. I know whereof I speak.

Like a clandestine meeting in the night, the craving conspired with the opportunity and the temptation was overwhelming. The curiosity grew to a desire, the desire to a lust and the lust to a craving, an insatiable craving, an all-consuming craving. That craving would see you utterly in ruin, financially destitute, morally and spiritually bankrupt and emotionally dead and still craving more! More sex, more porn, more prostitutes, more deviance. This time it has to be more risky. This time it has to be more elaborate. This time a blonde, this time a red head, this time older, this time younger until you find yourself doing those things you always swore you would never do.

> "Blessed is the man who remains steadfast under trial, for when he has stood the test he will receive the crown of life, which God has promised to those who love him. Let no one say when he is tempted, "I am being tempted by God," for God cannot be tempted with evil, and he himself tempts no one. But each person is tempted when he is lured and enticed by his own desire. Then desire when it has conceived gives birth to sin, and sin when it is fully grown brings forth death."
> James 1:12-15 ESV http://bible.com/59/jas.1.12-15.esv

I do not presume to know your specific troubles. I need not know the details of your colorful past or the number of notches in your belt or the number of broken hearts you have left behind. The enemy may use different tactics in different battles but the war remains the same and his spoils are always the hearts and souls of men and those who love them. When it comes to bondage you must be honest about the source of that bondage and the power of that bondage over you.

Who has the authority?

I want you to read the following story straight from the Word of God and then I will point out some significant things that you might overlook.

Dagon the fishy god…

"When the Philistines captured the ark of God, they brought it from Ebenezer to Ashdod. Then the Philistines took the ark of God and brought it into the house of Dagon and set it up beside Dagon. And when the people of Ashdod rose early the next day, behold, Dagon had fallen face downward on the ground before the ark of the Lord. So they took Dagon and put him back in his place. But when they rose early on the next morning, behold, Dagon had fallen face downward on the ground before the ark of the Lord, and the head of Dagon and both his hands were lying cut off on the threshold. Only the trunk of Dagon was left to him. This is why the priests of Dagon and all who enter the house of Dagon do not tread on the threshold of Dagon in Ashdod to this day. The hand of the Lord was heavy against the people of Ashdod, and he terrified and afflicted them with tumors, both Ashdod and its territory. And when the men of Ashdod saw how things were, they said, "The ark of the God of Israel must not remain with us, for his hand is hard against us and against Dagon our god." So they sent and gathered together all the lords of the Philistines and said, "What shall we do with the ark of the God of Israel?" They answered, "Let the ark of the God of Israel be brought around to Gath." So they brought the ark of the God of Israel there. But after they had brought it around, the hand of the Lord was against the city, causing a very great panic, and he afflicted the men of the city, both young and old, so that tumors broke out on them. So they sent the ark of God to Ekron. But as soon as the ark of God came to Ekron, the people of Ekron cried out, "They have brought around to us the ark of the God of Israel to kill us and our people." They sent therefore and gathered together all the lords of the Philistines and said, "Send away the ark of the God of Israel, and let it return to its own place, that it may not kill us and our people." For there was a deathly panic throughout the whole city. The hand of God was very heavy there. The men who did not die were struck with tumors, and the cry of the city went up to heaven."

1 Samuel 5:1-12 ESV

http://bible.com/59/1sa.5.1-12.esv

H7218

ראש rô'sh, roshe

From an unused root apparently meaning to shake; the head (as most easily shaken), whether literally or figuratively (in many applications, of place, time, rank, etc.): - band, beginning, captain, chapiter, chief (-est place, man, things), company, end, X every [man], excellent, first, forefront, ([be-]) head, height, (on) high (-est part, [priest]), X lead, X poor, principal, ruler, sum, top.

H3709

כף kaph, kaf

From H3721; the hollow hand or palm (so of the paw of an animal, of the sole, and even of the bowl of a dish or sling, the handle of a bolt, the leaves of a palm tree); figuratively power: - branch, + foot, hand ([-ful], -dle, [-led]), hollow, middle, palm, paw, power, sole, spoon.

Perhaps I am reading too much into this. But it seems to me to be obvious that this idol of fools was challenged to stand face to face with the one physical object on Earth at the time that embodied the very Holiness and power of God. The idol fell short! Twice! The second time not just falling short but falling to pieces. That to me is obvious. As I looked at this passage I quickly understood that the head might come off of any wimpy little god who could not so much as keep his balance, but when I read that his palms were cut off too I had to ask why and what is the statement God is trying to make.

The "Strong's" concordance seems to indicate that the head represented authority, lordship, a ruler and the palms symbolized the power. If I understand that right, God was telling this fishy little character that in HIS presence HE was the authority and had all the power. In your life God has all power and authority as well. He has power over your thoughts, your temptations your desires and your habits. There is nothing in your life God cannot control… except your will.

We all want to be believed not deceived. But if the way you think is filled with lies, you must repent of what you believe.

It is hard to accept this truth, but everyone has been fooled by someone. Harder still is understanding when the greatest liar in your life is you. Lies which make you feel vindicated, accepted or approved of are far too easy to believe. Lies which justify your behavior are far too easy to create. Lies which have been repeated by you and everyone you know are often accepted as a universal truth. This is a giant problem for the addict because most addicts hang out with other addicts, thus they all believe and repeat the same lies. Whether you have created the lie, bought into the lie, spread the lie or just lived by the lie, the impact to your soul and spiritual condition are the same. You are a slave to the lie.

The core principles you live your life by, the values you use in decision making and the skills you have mastered for relationship building will all be affected by the lies you believe. To find true freedom, you must re-center yourself around truth. A change in the way you receive and react to lies will be key to this lasting life change. If you seek to be free of your addiction and to be empowered to lead others to freedom, learning to change your thinking about lies is a top priority. Transformation is what you are longing for. Truth is the only way to find transformation.

Write out some of the lies you identified in section one. You should have a good starting list on page "Identify: Lies."

As you write the list this time, use a pencil or pen of a different color and write underneath each lie the truth you must replace it with as you change your mind about the lie.

BEHAVIORS

What is the toughest part of this fight we call spiritual warfare? Knowing who to swing at. The flesh is the natural center of our human behavior.

It is the nature of a dog to bark. I have not yet met a dog that could meow. It is not in their nature. It is the nature of the human body to be hungry, to thirst, to need companionship and to crave sexual intimacy. When I first began to understand that the nature of the flesh was uh, natural, I realized that there was something more that I must do if I was going to find victory. I could not just rail against the devil and expect him to run away with his tail between his legs. Besides, it was not always the devil causing me to do what I did. Sometimes I did it because I wanted to, because it felt good, because I thought I had to, because it was a habit that controlled me.

I could not JUST cry out to God and expect that all my troubles would vanish. I had to make some choices and then some decisions and then make a commitment to those decisions. Do you understand what I am saying? Have you ever decided to make a commitment? Perhaps to lose the holiday pounds by the end of January or to be svelte by the start of summer. But it is much easier to decide to make a commitment than it is to make a commitment to that decision and live up to that commitment. Confused yet? Good! That means you are actually paying attention. What I am saying is this. It is not enough to decide to change something, you have to be committed, dedicated, it has to be a do or die decision. If you are not willing to kill for freedom, you are destined to bondage. If you will not slay the flesh, you will not be free of him. Paul called it the body of death. Do a little history search on that ancient torture method. Wow!

There is no worse enemy in the world than a good friend gone bad. I mean really, who knows your weaknesses better? Who knows what hurts you and what you will fall for better than your best friend? Who knows when you are at your weakest moments? Who knows what motivates you to action and what your breaking point is? Who knows you better than yourself?

When you begin to succumb to this enemy, that proud arrogant fool that wants to rule the world anyway, you will find that he pulls out all the stops, bypasses all your defenses and leaves a wake of terror in your soul. He has NO CONCERN for the things of the spirit. He prefers war, he knows he has all the inside information and as long as you feed him, he is the strongest dog in the fight. Stop feeding him. Stop trusting him. Abandon the idea that you are friends.

"Beloved, I urge you as sojourners and exiles to abstain from the passions of the flesh, which wage war against your soul."
1 Peter 2:11 ESV http://bible.com/59/1pe.2.11.esv

"But I say, walk by the Spirit, and you will not gratify the desires of the flesh. For the desires of the flesh are against the Spirit, and the desires of the Spirit are against the flesh, for these are opposed to each other, to keep you from doing the things you want to do."
Galatians 5:16-17 ESV http://bible.com/59/gal.5.16-17.esv

There is a picture of this unbelievably mysterious yet formidable foe. Each day, when you shave, you look him in the face. The nature of the old man that once was you, before Christ came in, that is the one enemy that is hardest to eradicate. For victory to be true, sure and permanent in this war on sexual sin, that old man must die. He must be dragged kicking and screaming to the cross for execution. He cannot be tolerated another minute. Left alone he will destroy you.

Many churches and church leaders treat behavioral modification as the primary indicator to know repentance has taken place.

This is the place most people expect a book of this nature to begin or at least to focus most of the time and energy. It has been my experience both in my own life and in the life of those I have taught, trained and mentored as a Certified Leadership Coach, behavior almost always follows thought.

115

If the way you think is out of whack, your behavior will follow suit. If your thoughts are out of control, driven by lies, self-destructive or overly self-centered your behavior will be just the same.

All of the habit shifting, bouncing eyes, environmental controls, circles of friends, accountability partners, site blocking software, ankle monitors and secured financial access will not prevent you from acting out in your addiction because the sin is not first in the action, but in the soul, the mind. How do I know this? Let me show you in God's word.

There are a few passages which will spark your thinking about when and how sin begins and where God's judgement begins to call it sin.

Check out these passages, rewrite them in your own words and ask God what you need to repent of and journal His answers below.

Luke 6:45

Proverbs 6:25

Romans 2:5

Romans 8:6

Job 3:11

1 Corinthians 6:13

Matthew 5:28

WAY OF ESCAPE

Arising In Our Midst ~ by James L. Norris ~ 25 December 1991

Growing up is always a challenge. Growing up as a young man with no male role models is a bit harder. I look back on the many times my mouth nearly got me erased from existence and wonder if it was anything less than the Almighty Hand of God that protected me.

I recall a day in High School. I was a freshman and had quite an attitude on life because I basically had no one to tell me what to do. I had a crush on a young lady two grades higher than myself. Strangely enough she liked me too. Unfortunately, she was rather popular among the older guys and a few of them did not care for my interest in her.

One afternoon, I was in front of the school all alone waiting for my ride home when three guys confronted me. One of them had a crush on the same young lady I did. He made it clear to me that he had cared for her much longer and that if I didn't make myself scarce he would. I didn't find any logic behind what he said, nor did I find any logic in arguing with the three of them.

My mouth being what it was, it was hard for me to seem sincere, even in the face of terror. I told him I would stay away but I don't think he liked the way I worded my reply. He began to advance toward me. I was too scared to fight him, he was at least twice my size. I was also too stupid to run away, so I just stood there motionless. The closer he got the more of my life I saw flash before my eyes. He pulled out his knife. I wasn't crying yet, but I don't know why. Then, from out of nowhere, came a voice, a voice of thunder almost. I didn't know men's voices could be that low. I almost jumped when I heard it. The words he spoke were not for me to hear, I guess that's why I didn't understand a thing he said. The guy in front of me dropped his knife as a huge hand rested on my shoulder. I looked at that hand. I had no idea who he was or why he was on my side but I'm glad he was. The other guy apologized, grabbed his knife, said he was only joking and left.

I turned to see if I recognized the man behind me. I saw a belly button. It didn't look familiar. I looked up to a face I had never seen before in my life. He introduced himself as Matt, a friend of my sister's. My heart raced and for the first time in my life I realized I wasn't fighting this world all alone.

I have come to know the Lord as my personal Savior since that day. He has made me many promises about life, and life more abundantly, about eternal life and many more, but the two I hold dear are these: "I will be your friend and stick closer than a brother..." and "In your weakness I am strong!"

These two promises simply mean that I never have to face my enemies all alone. My best friend is there for me always, and most often He knows when I'll need Him long before I do.

There is a song that speaks of God's love for us. How he goes before us conquering all our enemies and placing them under His feet. To some, that song has little meaning because they either fight the battle themselves, or they never give God the credit for the victory. When I look back on the situations in my life that I couldn't have gotten out of with all my effort, and see a victory as the end result, I can't help but to rejoice in the fact that He is a Mighty Warrior, and He is Arising in our Midst.

"Be sober-minded; be watchful. Your adversary the devil prowls around like a roaring lion, seeking someone to devour. Resist him, firm in your faith, knowing that the same kinds of suffering are being experienced by your brotherhood throughout the world."
1 Peter 5:8-9 ESV http://bible.com/59/1pe.5.8-9.esv

"Put on the whole armor of God, that you may be able to stand against the schemes of the devil."
Ephesians 6:11 ESV http://bible.com/59/eph.6.11.esv

"For we do not wrestle against flesh and blood, but against the rulers, against the authorities, against the cosmic powers over this present darkness, against the spiritual forces of evil in the heavenly places."

Satan is not playing. He wants to eat you for lunch. The lion roars for two things, to run the young lions away from any kill they might have gotten that he wants to steal for himself and to intimidate any other lions from coming into his territory and taking his stolen spoils. Satan wants you to believe that he has all the power and authority. He is lying. He lost his right to rule when Jesus came back from the dead with the keys to death and Hell.

Now you say that you have no hope of overcoming this sin in your life. You say that the battle has been too long, that you are addicted and out of control. I say you are allowing your enemy to intimidate you into inaction. You have believed the lie that you cannot fight this, that you have no power and no authority. Hogwash!

"Beloved, do not believe every spirit, but test the spirits to see whether they are from God, for many false prophets have gone out into the world. By this you know the Spirit of God: every spirit that confesses that Jesus Christ has come in the flesh is from God, and every spirit that does not confess Jesus is not from God. This is the spirit of the antichrist, which you heard was coming and now is in the world already. Little children, you are from God and have overcome them, for he who is in you is greater than he who is in the world."
1 John 4:1-4 ESV http://bible.com/59/1jn.4.1-4.esv

If your father were the President of the US, you would have the Secret Service at your beck and call. Whom do you think is on stand-by being a child of the living God? The very angels of Heaven! He is the God of angel armies; the most powerful creatures of all time have been commissioned to not let any harm come to you. What foolish little fish god, or demon of lust or desire would walk into that battle with his eyes wide open? The same one you invited in and continue to sign a truce with every time he comes to plunder your life, that's who. He does not fear your army, he doesn't expect you to call on them.

How many times will you promise yourself, your spouse you will never look at pornography again? How many times will you pray and cry for God to deliver you from your addiction while you hold one last trick behind your back? How many stolen glances will become stares, then sinful meditation then outright lust? How many sanctions must he violate, no fly zones must he cross, innocents must he kill before you declare war? God has given you a way out. You must take action.

My friend it is time to admit the tag up. You are the wrestler in the ring being pummeled by both of your opponents. It is time wake up to the fact that you have bitten off more than you can chew. There are rules to this fight but your opponent does not play by them, neither has he the intention of letting you go when you cry uncle. He is bent on your destruction and your very soul is his trophy. You will not win if you play by the same rules you have always played by.

It is time my friend to TAG UP! Fall on your knees, admit your failure and your inability, and perhaps even unwillingness to fight. Cry out to God for help. He will hear you. He will send help. When you reach for the ropes and stretch out your arm; the very brush of that nail-scarred hand is the deafening blow of your enemy's demise.

More densely populated than any other prison system in the world, humans are incarcerated by their own thoughts.

Excuses are a powerful deterrent to success. The ability of an addict to cast blame and deflect responsibility are second to none. In the height of addiction, it is even possible if not probable for God to get the blame.

"God gave me these cravings."

"God made me like this."

"I was born this way."

These ideas have become so commonly acceptable, they have even been made into popular songs. Are you challenged with taking responsibility for your own choices and consequences? Do you find yourself blaming others for the negative outcomes of your addictive behavior or even for the cravings themselves? Do you look at the options you were given to walk away from those choices and realize how many times you could have been free but chose not to be?

Remember in this segment of the book we are talking about a "change of thinking" which leads to a change of behavior and a transformed life. The promise from God to always provide you a way of escape is quite significant. If you are unwilling to look for this way out, or you are unaware when the way out is provided, you will continue to be a "victim" of your own thinking and socially separated from those who want to see you free.

> "No temptation has overtaken you that is not common to man. God is faithful, and he will not let you be tempted beyond your ability, but with the temptation he will also provide the way of escape, that you may be able to endure it."
> 1 Corinthians 10:13 ESV http://bible.com/59/1co. 10.13.esv

The mark on the side of the boat which tells the load master when the ship has been overloaded is called a "flim-saw line." When this line reaches the water's surface, the load master will cease the cargo distribution on the ship because it is literally more than the ship can bear. One more article loaded could be the proverbial straw that broke the camel's back and the ship will sink. In your life, God knows what you can bear.

While God is in no way the one tempting you or causing the temptation to come, He will absolutely intervene before you are overwhelmed, and offer options for you to choose another route. God will not tamper with your will nor override it. If you refuse to accept the way of escape or fail to identify it, you may continue on your way deeper into sin and destruction.

You must change the way you think about God's offer to avoid sin. Sadly, this offer will not likely come with hi-way signs which read "last free exit" or "You are entering the tollway" but signs will always be available if you are aware.

Most of the "ways of escape" in your life will be more easily recognized in hindsight. Meditate on the moments of failure when you gave in to temptation recently.

Write out some of the moments you can recognize now as offers God made for you to stop the process of temptation.

CONSEQUENCES

There is a truth to all consequences. They are unavoidable short of mercy.

To repent of consequences might seem a contradiction or even heresy at first glance. When you apply the truest meaning of "repent" meaning a change of mind and thought, which leads to a change of heart and behavior, you can understand better. What I want you to consider is this; consequences are often the tool of a loving father who wants the very best for you.

Consequences may be punitive, judgment carried out by men such as rehab, incarceration, termination of employment, removal of privileges or access or even the end of a treasured relationship by divorce. Consequences may also be the natural course of events such as permanent damage to your health as in a destroyed liver, diseases transmitted sexually or through sharing of needles.

Consequences are imminent without the intervention of grace. Consequences are frightening. Consequences of sin are undesirable in most cases. Consequences can even be the judgement of God as was the case many times in the Old Testament.

However, consequences do not mean God has stopped loving you. Consequences do not mean God has disowned you. Consequences do not mean grace is not sufficient for you. Consequences do not mean God no longer plans to speak to you, embrace you or use you.

When you think properly about your consequences, your heart will have the ability to hold on to hope and to cherish the grace which means your sin debt has been paid and your eternity is covered. The price paid by Jesus on the cross did not erase consequences in this life, but it more than covered the consequences of death and the grave. If you have a living and loving relationship with the person of Jesus Christ, the incarnation of God, you have all you need to live life everlasting, resurrected to glory.

Take a moment to re-read Romans 8:1 and write the verse in your own words using the space below.

Consequences, good or bad are tools for influencing thoughts and behaviors.

When you think of consequences as only negative, it is hard to submit yourself to learn from them. You will need to change your thinking about consequences if you want to find freedom from your addiction.

Understanding how a loving father would allow pain to come for the value of a lesson capable of preventing greater pain and understanding some of the pain you are enduring is purely self-inflicted is necessary. You have thought and behaved in such a way as to experience these consequences. Not every negative consequence is the result of some outside or demonic influence, right?

Accepting the punishment due to you is a large part of maturity. Young children often cannot accept the blame even if they were alone in the causing of the problem.

I once read of a young man asked to keep his nephew for a few hours while mom went to the store. At one point the toddler came to the door of the room and said very clearly to his uncle, "Someone pooped in my pants!" The misery and uncomfortable sensation which must come with having poop in your pants is bad enough, the idea that someone else has "done it to you" must be unbearable humiliation.

As you pray, take ownership of your own consequences. There is nothing wrong with asking the consequences to be removed or lessened. There is also no promise it will happen. In either case, your loving Father will be faithfully by your side every step of the way, if you allow it.

Take a moment to write out some of the consequences you have endured which you previously blamed on others.

TRUTH

Truth is indisputable even though this statement is not. Truth is not subject to your thinking, but your thoughts must be subjected to truth.

One of the hardest things you must change to find freedom is the submission of your will. To repent of truth is a bit of an oxymoron to average thinking. Perhaps you have heard someone claim, "That's your truth but its not my truth." This loose definition of truth is exactly the problem and the reason we need to change the way we think about truth.

Like gravity, truth is not relative. The law of gravity holds zero regard for your religious persuasion, your political ideologies, your race, national origin, sexual orientation or education level. When you drop a bowling ball on your foot, it falls down every time, not up or sideways. This truth is indisputable. Gravity is a law.

The law of sin and death is another truth which will not regard any man or woman for their pedigree. When God declares His ways just and His judgement of sin to be indisputable, only a fool calls God a liar. The price to be paid for disregarding this truth is heavy, hot and everlasting. The truth of Hell is just as real and imminent a destination for those who deny Christ, who has been mocked, derided, denied, ridiculed and literally laughed at, as it is for those who wish to hold God only to the standards of grace and mercy.

Listen to me closely. If there is no punishment for sin and rebellion, there is no justice. If there is no justice, there is no need for grace and mercy because all are equal. In such a scenario, an unrepentant mass murderer and my brand new baby granddaughter or grandson are seen as equal before the judgement seat. Where is the justice in that? (Yes I believe in original sin.)

It is so easy to get caught up in the thoughts of your addiction and forget you are loved. It is easy to see yourself as unlovable. It is easy to believe the lie, "you are what you do." Even if Forest Gump did say "Stupid is as stupid does." You are not defined by your behavior. You are defined by your being. If you are born again, you are a new creature in Christ and you need to begin to think like He thinks.

Repenting of "truth" is a continuation of changing your perception about reality. What you see is truly less real than what God says is true. "Seeing is believing" is a popular phrase but it leaves out the aspect of faith which requires you to see with the eyes of your heart not the eyes of your head.

You will really need to challenge your own convictions. You will need to question everything you say you believe to be true. You will need to spend more time in God's Word and in prayerful conversation with Him to re-establish your connection to Truth. Truth is not an idea, a problem to be solved, a solution to be discovered. Truth is a person who has covered you, embraced you even in your worst failures and made a way for you to spend the rest of eternity with Him in paradise. Taking time to get to know Him will forever transform you.

Take a few minutes and just ask Truth to reveal himself to you on a whole new level and to help you to think about Him as you should.

Your thinking is so critical to your freedom and your success in this battle against your addiction, I do not want to tell you what to think. I want you to challenge TRUTH himself and ask Him to tell you what to think. I am going to give you a few prompts to start your thinking and give you some probing questions to seek answers to which I believe will change your mind and transform your life.

Write the responses you receive as you pray for deep truth to be revealed about the following notions:

a) Purity of Heart

b) Godly Wisdom

c) Freedom from guilt and condemnation

d) Freedom from sin

REASON TO FIGHT

When you don't know what you're fighting for, you will not fight the right enemy, with the right priorities, passion or power.

I was napping on a late Sunday afternoon. As we snuggled there on the bed together, I fell into a deeper sleep and began to dream of an encounter with a mugger on the street. In the dream, he was trying to take her from me, and hurt the one I loved. As I am sure you have experienced, I struggled as if in quicksand. I yelled but as if through a pillow. I tried to fight back. I tried to intimidate the mugger and nothing seemed to be working. Suddenly, I threw an uppercut with all my might. I intended to take this fool's head off his shoulders. I felt the force of my body tightening, every muscle fiber was redirected from my big toe, through my hips, core, bicep and shoulder. It landed! No quicksand this time! BAM!

I was awakened by her sobbing...

I struggled in my sleep against an imaginary foe. I fought in this real world and landed a punch you couldn't pay me enough to throw. She had a bruise on her chin for a few days. I had a broken and contrite heart for months. Even now, many years later, I am filled with regret for that moment. It makes me nauseous to recall.

In the beginning of this segment of the book, I told you how my first priority was my addiction. You will have to be deeply honest with yourself to admit the same. Until you do, you will wrestle with the wrong opponents. In fact, if you are not consciously aware of your surroundings, you will find yourself fighting more with those you love than with the elements of destruction bent on your personal demise.

To repent of your reason to fight, is to refocus your attention, your effort, your combativeness, your warrior tactics, your best strategies away from family and friends onto the enemy of your soul and your own internal desires.

Now is a good time to concentrate on the battles raging in your mind. The thoughts which cause you to shift blame. The interruptions which cause you to explode with anger. Realize in this moment how many of those interruptions, those infuriating phone calls, text messages, honey-do requests were also a gracious and mighty God doing everything in His power to get your attention and redirect your will. In Balaam's life, he used a donkey. See 2 Peter 2:15-16

Write at least one thought which has changed how you perceive your circumstances, victims, and enemies.

Let's Be Real

To help understand the pain God feels
Please put yourself in His place
Understand what part of life is real
And the power of God's forgiving grace

The Lord created man to worship Him
He created them with their own free will
Knowing they would deny Him within
And knowing they would kill

When man turned away from God's light
he followed Satan to his dark domain
So God sent His only Son, Jesus Christ
Who, it seems, only died in vain

He tried to offer the world a chance
To accept His redeeming grace
But the world ran to Satan's hand
And slapped the Lord in the face

The world condemned this Child of God
They murdered Him in cold, innocent blood
Apparently they forgot the Wrath of God
How He destroyed the world by flood

Remember a moment how God must feel
After rebuilding an empty world
Put the pain of God to something real
And live that pain once more

If standing beside your family
Facing uncertain death
You'd offer your life that they be freed
Knowing that you'd be dead

Yet after you were left to die
And you lay dying in your own blood
The killer took your family's lives
You'd realize your death was no good

Now you know how Christ died in vain
Giving His life to save the world
Now you know His eternal pain
When you say He is no more

You should praise the Lord for His love for you
And remember each day of your life
The cross still stands as living proof
Of God's promise you don't have to die

4/18/1990

As you can see from the date, this notion of fighting in vain has been heavy on my heart for more than 35 years. I know you have different trigger points than I do, things which set you off to fight back. Could you imagine even for a moment how God feels?

He gave His very best for you. He gave his only begotten Son. When you live as if you have no power to fight, you mock His death. Is your mind made up to fight for purity, for

135

holiness, for Christlikeness? Sure, your initial motivations to resist the temptation of your addiction might first be found in family, friends, career or ministry at risk, but ultimately, God is concerned with your relationship to Him more than anything else.

About the same time I wrote the poem above I was spending time off base with a few people from a small church in England. They had a cook out and invited several people from the base and the neighboring community. I met a fistful of new friends that day. A couple of them I still chat with on Facebook from time to time. One young man in particular engaged me in a serious conversation about faith. He was not yet a follower of Christ, but he is a very smart guy and was filled with challenging questions.

As we wrapped up our conversation I remember telling him, "There are two promises of God you need to be aware of. You will not find them written exactly this way in scripture, but I know them to be true in the context of many, many Bible stories and in my own experience. First, if there is anything in your life which means more to you than God, get a good look at it, you are guaranteed to lose it. God will play second fiddle behind no one and no thing. Second, If God has to break your legs to get you on your knees in prayer, expect your legs to be broken. He loves you that much and He wants to fellowship with you."

Only 24 hours later, the same man was outside my dorm screaming my name. When I came out to see what was wrong, he asked me to drive him to the emergency room on base. The whole time he was crying and just kept asking, "How did you know?" He had a fight with "the love of his life". His fiancé broke-off the engagement and while chasing her from the NCO Club, he stepped on a parking stop and hyper-extended his knee to the point he couldn't walk on it. He was convinced that I had "spoken this over him" and caused it to happen. Nope.

I just know the effort a father will exert to rescue his children. It's certainly better to have one eye in heaven, than two eyes in hell.

If your thought process right now leads you to believe God will not intervene in your addiction. Think again. Repent of what you are fighting for, and begin to fight for the same thing your Heavenly Father wants. You will have much more synergy in the battle.

WRONG THOUGHTS

Perhaps at one time you have left a baby bottle on the counter overnight with a wee bit of milk in the bottom. When you return to use the bottle again you find the milk is dried to the bottom. Try as you might, no bottlebrush, no dishwasher, no amount of soap will remove the milk from the bottle. Perhaps you, like I have resorted to the butter knife and dishcloth, no luck! Finally you discard the bottle with no hope of using it again.

Let's pretend you left an ounce or two of milk in the bottle, not overnight but for say twenty or twenty-five years. Now you set the bottle in the sink and fill it full of crystal clear, fresh, cold, filtered water. Would you then give the bottle to your baby, a friend's baby or even an enemy's baby? I pray not! The milk, now green with mold and clabbered is like mud, full of bacteria and all sorts of yucky stuff. It is fit for no human. You would not dare submit someone to such a potential health hazard.

The bottle is your heart. The clabbered milk like yuck in the bottom is the pain and failures of your past. Once it is settled there it takes something significant to remove it. To fill the bottle to the top will only contaminate the filtered water. To scrape around in the milky water only loosens the stuff to be floaters in the water. You can dig with the knife, scrub with the brush, shake the bottle and scour it in the dishwasher until it changes shape. But no amount of therapy, no amount of self-pity, remorse or self-loathing will break free the crud. These wrong thoughts of self are too deeply embedded.

What is the solution to wrong thoughts?

Write your ideas in the space below.

RIGHT THOUGHTS

What overcomes wrong thoughts? Right thoughts!

Ironically, to place the nasty bottle in the sink, under the tap, whether a steady but incessant drip or a mighty rushing flow of fresh cold water, the bottle will at once be filled, then filled to overflowing, then the constant in-flow of water will have an eroding effect on the crud until it breaks it up. Time is still the key. A constant flow is a powerful tool, the crud now broken, will float to the top and down the drain, never to be seen again.

Whether your heart is filled with the pain inflicted on you or the pain of your own failures and past mistakes, take heart!

The water is yours for the taking; it flows from an endless well. It is the water of eternal life. Jesus says if you drink of this well you will never thirst again. Get your heart in the path of the Glory of God, seek Him in worship and grow in your faith in Him through the WORD.

As you live your life at any stage in the purification process, be cautious what you have in your bottle (the thoughts and words in your heart). There are too many shattered lives, hearts who may never be returned to God because someone got just enough of The Word in them to become proud and judgmental. To serve in ministry while the failures of the past are still ruling your emotions and thoughts is to serve to an infant the murky, cloudy, floaty filled water which has not yet been purified.

Praise God we live in the age of grace. If our Heavenly Father can speak through a donkey, He can use me, even me. Just remember His promise. His Word will never return to Him void. Speak The Truth in love, speak His Word and His alone and no harm shall come to those in need, regardless the current condition of your heart.

Heed this word of caution to not let spiritual pride and arrogance lead you to hurt someone else in need of Christ and at the same time, the confidence to do as you are called with no excuse that you are not yet ready.

> "Remind them to be submissive to rulers and authorities, to be obedient, to be ready for every good work, to speak evil of no one, to avoid quarreling, to be gentle, and to show perfect courtesy toward all people. For we ourselves were once foolish, disobedient, led astray, slaves to various passions and pleasures, passing our days in malice and envy, hated by others and hating one another. But when the goodness and loving kindness of God our Savior appeared, he saved us, not because of works done by us in righteousness, but according to his own mercy, by the washing of regeneration and renewal of the Holy Spirit,

so that being justified by his grace we might become heirs according to the hope of eternal life. The saying is trustworthy, and I want you to insist on these things, so that those who have believed in God may be careful to devote themselves to good works. These things are excellent and profitable for people."
Titus 3:1-5, 7-8 ESV http://bible.com/59/tit.3.1-5,7-8.esv

WHO YOU HURT

When you have been a victim, it is hard to imagine hurting others. The truth is, hurt people, hurt people.

The thoughts which dominate the mind of the addict are seldom focused on the wellbeing of others. You know too well how easy it is to settle in to the selfish demands of your addiction. When your needs are not being met, the blame is more than enough to cast on everyone in your path. An addict will blame family, friends, neighbors, random strangers, traffic lights, computer viruses, the economy and even the weather. Do you know who you as an addict will not blame? Yup, yourself!

Again, I am not pointing fingers in a direction I have not stood first. I shifted the blame, focused my anger and frustration on everyone else and took no responsibility for my actions, behaviors or consequences until God changed the way I thought about my addiction and the pain it brought on those I love.

Repentance in this arena is a painful process. It means taking responsibility for all the stupid, painful and destructive words you have ever uttered. Repentance here means aligning yourself with the way God hears and reacts to your fits and outbursts. You will not find freedom for your addiction if your will cannot be surrendered. Your will cannot be surrendered if you remain convinced of your innocence and everyone else's guilt in your downfall. I am leaving you plenty of space on this page to write a personal apology to the person or persons who have been the focus of your rage, the victims of your addiction. It's time to change the way you think about them. It's time to change how you see them in your minds eye. Write out your apology and include the contrast - the way you have perceived them in the past against the way you are committing to perceiving them from now on. (Whether the person ever sees this or not is between you and God, be sure to ask him.)

SUMMARY & ACTION

Action trumps everything. Taking action on the thoughts you allow in your mind cannot be ignored.

In my opinion, the best example of true repentance can be found in 2 Corinthians 10:5-6. Your thoughts rest in your mind. Your mind is 1/3 of your soul along with will and emotions. The area of human existence which God will influence but not control is the will of man. Your will is not the responsibility of God. He will love you. He will guide you. He will cherish you. He will protect you. He will chasten and correct you. He will not control your will. Your choices are under your control.

When you choose to fight, God will fight along-side you. When you resist the devil, he will flee. God will see to it. When you take every stray, destructive, addictive thought captive and force it to obey Christ, the power of the cross will break the chains of your slavery to sin and set you free. The price for everlasting life has been paid. The price for abundant living is paid moment by moment in your choices and in the thoughts you choose to think.

Add a page or two into the book for this exercise. Write down every wrong, addictive and destructive thought which begs for attention and shelf space in your mind for the next ten days.

FORGIVE

Forgiveness is the most powerful expression of unconditional love known to mankind, a choice to not hold against them an account of their misdeeds.

SIN

The sin in me cursed my relationships, broke hearts and weakened minds. Forgiveness redeemed what sin destroyed.

Sin is separation from God and others which expresses itself in your addiction, but it is more than poor choices, more than bad behavior, more than wrong thoughts. Sin is the nature of a man or woman without God, so forgiveness through Christ is the only way you can be reconciled to God. Changing your behavior is a great and needed choice. Changing your thoughts and attitudes about your sin are absolutely needed as well. However, without forgiveness, there is no restoration or reconciliation.

We have discussed sin at length in this book. Sin hurts others, destroys dreams, goals, relationships, faith and more. We need a cure for sin. We need freedom from the bondage of sin. Repentance and confession work together to call sin what it is and change the way we think about sin. For true freedom to begin, we need to know the price has been paid for more than behavioral modification. The price can only be paid by death, so Jesus paid it for us. If you have not been reconciled to Christ through a verbal confession of sin and acknowledgment of His Lordship over your life, turn to the last page of this book and read aloud the prayer provided for you. This confession of faith is the key to reconcile with the Father for the forgiveness of sin.

Next you need to consider a quite difficult concept; forgiving yourself. The idea of forgiveness is expected to be pointed at someone else. Whether you are asking God to forgive you, or you are struggling to forgive those who have hurt you, forgiveness always seems to be about others.

I can tell you from experience, forgiving me was the hardest thing to do. I know God says it is finished. I know Jesus paid the price for my sin. I know He now sees me as righteous and justified. In the words of some preachers, "Justified means, just as if I'd never sinned." But I know what I have done wrong better than anyone else. I deal with the haunting memories. I confront the thoughts and take them captive far too often. As James Robison said recently, "At 73 years old and 55 years in ministry I know this... The enemy never retires." I have good reason to hate me. Except...

There was a day when I was particularly hating myself. Looking back on my life and all the wasted years, thinking how I have so little to offer and so much to regret for all the wrong I've done. When I spoke the words which were running through my mind, the Father asked me a stinging question about all the things I held against myself.

"If the cross was sufficient for my Holiness to see past your sin, what authority do you have to hold your sin against yourself?" A few years later He reminded me, "You're not yet doing what I called you to do because you still hate you

more than you love those I have called you to serve."
Forgiving me was harder than forgiving those who brought
the greatest pain in my life. Forgiving me takes more daily
commitment, more conscious awareness, more diligence and
more grace than any other relationship in my life.

How my wife has forgiven me is truly beyond my human
comprehension. TransformingGrace.TV was born of this
revelation: her love, like God's love, to see past my failures
and pain inducing, addiction driven, foolish behavior, have
transformed me into a new creature.

Forgiveness does more for the human soul than to reconcile
the spirit. Forgiveness has a biochemical impact. It releases
stress, fights off depression, resists the temptation of
bitterness and gives a new perspective of the one forgiven. If
you really want to go deep on forgiveness consider this:
quantum physics entanglement theory states we are all
connected and no matter the separation of time and space,
energy of thought focused on a specific person can impact
them even to the level of their DNA. The old phrase offers
this: "bitterness is like drinking poison and expecting the
other person to die." What if your lack of forgiveness did
cause health problems for someone else? Is that what you
want? What if not forgiving yourself could cause health
problems for you?

When forgiveness becomes second nature, the clarity with
which you see life will be amazing. When you learn to let go
of the pain, the misunderstanding, the foolishness of

humanity, you will experience a new found freedom like never before. You will see all people with new eyes. You will become quick to forgive and slow to take offense. I know, it is happening to me more each day.

Use the rest of this page to consider honestly the people who your forgiveness could transform.

Who am I holding something against whom God has already paid the price for?

How is a lack of forgiveness causing me to feel when I think of them?

What has the lack of forgiveness done to our relationship?

Read Matthew 6:14-15 and write it here in your own words.

LIES

Lies are hard to detect, harder still to accept. Lies are hard to forgive, harder still to forget.

When you have been lied to and the truth exposes the lie, it is hard to trust again. Trust is the fabric of any relationship, without it a relationship cannot really flourish. Sure, an abusive relationship can be built on lies and manipulation. A narcissist can build dozens of relationships around a fabricated reality. As an addict, you likely have burned a few bridges, destroyed a few relationships and left a trail of distrust behind a life of many lies.

You have lied to you. You have lied to friends. You have lied to family. In all probability you have lied to total strangers. Think about it. Can you recall a time you spoke what you knew was not true, to someone who could not care less about the lie you told, or even what the real truth might have been?

As you begin this long journey of healing from addiction, you will need to consider making amends where possible and practical. Remember this segment under Confession. If asking for forgiveness or confessing to someone you lied to will only expose them to more pain, or pain they managed to avoid thus far, then take it to God and let Him advise you on things better left unsaid.

You also need to look deep inside and ask yourself about the reason you have lied to you for so long. Confront the excuses, the blame shifting, the escape from reality you have chosen as your lifestyle. Ask yourself about things you have believed and consider the ideas you need to release. Some of those ideas have caused you harm. Some of those ideas have cost you a great deal in finances, relationships or personal pain. The longer you hold on to those lies and keep telling them to yourself, the longer before you can let them go and forgive yourself.

Finally, forgiveness will require looking back to those who have lied to you. Perhaps it was a web of lies which exposed you to your addiction to begin with. Perhaps it was the perpetuation of lies which kept you in the cycle of your addiction. Either way, the lies will keep you in bondage until you give them up to God and let them go.

Know this, judgement, revenge, retaliation are all the purview of the Almighty. he shares that role with no one. If you feel like to have something to hold against anyone, including your victimizer or even yourself, you are mistaken.

BEHAVIORS

Behavior is a combination of all the acts you perform. Forgiveness is first an act, then a habit and eventually a behavior.

Until you understand how your behavior impacts the people around you it's really hard for you to perceive a need for forgiveness. The impact caused by other people's behavior in your life has left scars, pain and confusion or hope, healing and direction. If you were to guess, which do you think you left more of in other people's lives?

You have so far identified behavior, confessed behavior, and repented of behavior, now you are actually in a position to forgive behavior. Earlier you looked up a verse about how forgiveness was required of you for you to be forgiven. This is not a trick or manipulation on the part of God. I believe one of the worst and most hurtful sins we can commit as humans is the failure or outright refusal to forgive.

The human desire for revenge drives the gun violence in Chicago even though most of the larger gangs are long since gone. The drive for revenge for past hurts drives wedges which tear families apart. The drive for revenge is really nothing more than man doing what Satan did from the very beginning, demanding to share the rights to rule with God.

Sure, your addictive behavior was atrocious, vile, disgusting, disrespectful, and unbelievable painful, but if God no longer holds it against you, you have no right to either. Living under the belief your sin is too great is really living under the belief His blood was not sufficient for you.

You have no right to hold or execute judgement against the behavior anyone else has perpetrated against you, including you. Understand, I am not talking about the natural consequences or laws of the land, or the eventual punishment to be endured by an unrepentant heart. I am talking about you learning to let God be God. Stop judging yourself.

The sooner you learn to follow the steps repeatedly and rapidly, the sooner they become a habit:

1. Identify the harmful behavior, yours or someone else's.

2. Confess the harmful behavior (call it what God calls it, wickedness and sin).

3. Repent of your addiction and any other sinful behavior by changing your mind, taking every tempting thought captive and submitting it to the thought of Christ.

4. Forgive the behavior just as God has forgiven the behavior - you are not your judge or anyone else's.

WAY OF ESCAPE

If you were handed the escape route from a burning building and stood still screaming in pain, you would be a fool.

It is unbelievable how many people find themselves in the throws of addiction while they ignore a bright future filled with joy and hope calling out to them. The greatest way of escape from addiction is forgiveness. God's forgiveness must be accepted and acted on. Like the escape route, having it in your hands is awesome, but standing still and staring at it while your flesh burns is pointless.

Through scripture Jesus has reached out to you time and time again. His voice is constantly calling you in your dreams. His hands are outstretched to embrace you. His blood is dripping past the darkest mistakes you have ever made washing them clean from sin. He is waiting. Will you stand still or run to Him?

This is your chance to dance in freedom. This is your chance to run from your pain filled past. This is your chance to lean in to the Father's heart and to escape addiction at last.

Now its your turn to let the demons go who held your captors. Forgive those who hurt you and escape the bondage of judgment. It too is an addiction. Take heart they will be held to account in this life or the next, but your freedom rests it letting them go.

The most dangerous thing to know about a way of escape it this: it is mostly stationary. It may show up in many places and on many occasions of temptation but a way of escape will not hunt you down and set you free. You must move in the direction of the escape. The action is yours to take.

Can you see all the times your life could have been different if you had made a habit of forgiveness early on?

Can you bravely list things you have done but not released to God with a request for His forgiveness?

Can you list some hidden grudges you are still secretly cherishing as you wish ill against someone who wronged you?

This is a way of escape. This forgiveness will free you by releasing them.

CONSEQUENCES

Everyone will pay the piper eventually. In the debt of sin and death, the piper is paid in full. A lack of forgiveness has it's own piper.

In previous sections you read about the power of repentance and forgiveness working together to change your mind about someone else's wrong doings and to let them go form your judgement.

You also read how forgiveness is an act of attitude. (thought + emotion = attitude)

You also read how feelings and thoughts can effect your mind, body, health and spirit.

Dr. Caroline Leaf says:

> **"75% to 95% of the illnesses that plague us today are a direct result of our thought life.**
> What we think about affects us physically and emotionally. It's an epidemic of toxic emotions.
>
> The average person has over 30,000 thoughts a day. Through an uncontrolled thought life, we create the conditions for illness; we make ourselves sick! Research shows that fear, all on its own, triggers more than 1,400 known physical and chemical responses and activates more than 30 different hormones.

There are INTELLECTUAL and MEDICAL reasons to FORGIVE! Toxic waste generated by toxic thoughts causes the following illnesses: diabetes, cancer, asthma, skin problems and allergies to name just a few. Consciously control your thought life and start to detox your brain!"

Can you imagine missing out on the quality of life you deserve because you chose to not let go of the pain cycle in your life started by another?

Can you imagine leaving such a curse of ill health, mentally or physically on someone you love?

Can you imagine how many people you pass on the street everyday who are suffering with their own emotional dragons who could be free by someone simply forgiving them, or them receiving the forgiveness of Christ?

What are some of the intellectual and medical conditions in your life which might be attributed to a failure to forgive?

TRUTH

Forgiven

My heart leapt as I closed my eyes

My breath escaped me and I began to cry.

I felt the tears of pain inside my heart

And I repented that I'd missed the mark.

I felt once more like a failure,

I was right where I'd been before.

I had the fear of hurting God,

But not enough to make me stop.

Then as if from no where, I heard Him speak.

Was it real? Was He talking to me?

His voice was soft but firm

Not like anything I'd ever heard.

He said, "I love you child because you are mine

Not for what you have done

You're always loved in My Eyes

Because I loved my Son."

"He bled for you before He died.

So I have forgiven all your sin."

I thanked Him as I realized,

I was made whole in Him.

J. L. Norris 9-93

Need I say more?

REASON TO FIGHT

Complacency may be a greater enemy to healing than is judgement, Complacency is by definition, "content to a fault."

You must never let your guard down when it comes to sin. The one thing more addicting than chemicals or sex is the sensation of control, the lust for power. I know this doesn't sound anything like complacent. Will you think for a moment how to feels when you dramatically win a tough competition? Do you remember the high? Do you remember the utter flood of emotions which simultaneously said inside you, "I can't believe I won" and "I knew I could win all along?" When you are on top of your game and all foes are vanquished you are in great danger.

Forgiveness should be a great cry of mercy, grace and humility. It also demands from you the deepest commitment to remain in humility. Haughtiness loves a smug heart which shouts silently, "I have forgiven you for what you've done to me. You can't control me anymore. HA! Winning!"

STAND FIRM. Forgive. Then forgive again. Then again. Seven times seventy times a day, let it go. Your sins and the sin of others must be forgiven. The moment you feel like you have done all the forgiving you need to do, repent, and ask for forgiveness again.

Remember the enemy does not want you to be free. When you conquer your addiction, he will attack your pride. When you think you have conquered the left hook of pride, look for the uppercut, it's coming.

There is a high probability you have an assignment from Heaven which threatens the enemy. While he cannot tell the future, nor can he read minds, he can read patterns and he has been doing it well for centuries of human history. From the patterns in your family and spiritual make up, you have a reputation already in the heavenly realms. You may have seems signs before now to indicate you have not been under attack for no reason, but because the enemy needs to take you out or face major damage.

The reason you need to fight may look like a stranger in a foreign nation to you right now. In eternity, they may be their fruit of your victory over addiction. Forgiveness is one of the very few spiritual victories with resounding impact in both the physical and spiritual world.

If before this moment, you did not realize the grudges you were carrying held power to block the accomplishment your heavenly assignment while on this earth, you can no longer claim ignorance. You need to comprehend this: others relationships, lives, eternity may be hanging in the balance of your freedom. If you won't fight the fight of forgiveness for your own peace, fight for them.

WRONG THOUGHTS

Let it go! The wrong thought processes have not brought you peace, power or promise. Stop chasing them!

The world's way of thinking, likely the most prevalent way of thinking in your life, has been directed at "your rights" and privileges. You have more than likely been thought how to hold people to account for the way you feel. "Look how you made me feel," is a common idea today. Safe space, trigger words, guarded "free speech" and limited access for new thoughts and ideas are the norm on college campuses.

Forgiveness is a silly notion in this environment. If you consider forgiving someone who says a word or shares an idea you have opportunity to take offense at, you have betrayed the public trust. You are expected to castigate them in the town square, to bring them up on trial in the court of public opinion and if you have access to media, you must expose their error to the world. But under no circumstances do you forgive a politically incorrect statement or deed of ideology. Such behavior will not be tolerated in you.

Friends, this is not right, and it is not working. Looking for offense is a dangerous, harmful and destructive choice. John Bevere calls it the Bait of Satan. His book on this subject would be very helpful for you. I highly recommend it. Here is the Amazon description of the book itself.

> Escape the enemy's deadly trap! The Bait of Satan exposes one of the most deceptive snares Satan uses to get believers out of the will of God-offense. Most people who are ensnared by the bait of Satan don't even realize it. Don't be fooled! You will encounter offense, and it's up to you how it will affect your relationship with God. Your response will determine your future. If offense is handled correctly, you will become stronger rather than bitter. In this tenth anniversary edition of his best-selling book, John Bevere shows you how to stay free from offense and escape the victim mentality.

The victim mentality is a wrong thought. Revenge is a wrong thought. Demanding you own way is a wrong thought, not to mention immature, toddler like behavior.

You have already been encouraged to identify the wrong thoughts in your life, to confess them, and to repent of them. You are at a different level now. Letting go should be immediate. Take the thought of offense captive and beat it into submission to Christ instantly when it raises its ugly head. Offense only wants to strip you of power and authority. Instant forgiveness without condition is the most potent antidote to the venom of offense and victim hood.

Forgive now. Forgive quickly.

Forgive repeatedly. Forgive perpetually.

RIGHT THOUGHTS

To Come to The Throne ~ J Loren Norris

Tears filled my eyes as I searched my heart for the fear I felt. I wanted so desperately to just walk up to him after all this time, throw my arms around him and call him Father. My life had not been what I would have liked. My past still haunts me sometimes, especially the parts I can't seem to let go.

I walked ahead. All the while, my physical body moving boldly forward, my heart, my thoughts running away from me in fear. I knew he was my father. I knew he would love me no matter what I had done if he really loved me at all.

I walked into the room. It was full of people. Men and women from all over the world were gathered here. Just as I walked in the door, something inside me caused me to turn around. I turned in fear, almost startled to find no one behind me. My heart raced. I walked backward a few steps, then resumed my posture and carried on.

For what seemed like hours, I searched every face in the room; young to old, wealthy to poor, the strong, the weak, and anyone whose eyes I could get to match mine. I began to lose hope. The train would be leaving soon. If I didn't find him here, he would fade off into life and I may never have a chance like this again. First call rang through the station with a sense of urgency. People began to move to their boarding locations. I began to head for the exit. Nearly all hope was lost, then I saw him. He sat near the door I came in. He must have been there when I looked behind me. But I missed him as I turned to face the unexplained fear. We held each other in a warm embrace, tears filled every eye that looked on. Hearts raced and problems melted into understanding.

To think that I was in the same room for so long, wandering, wondering, and nearly missed the most glorious moment of my life to some fear of the past, of what lies behind, almost makes me sick.

For years men and women have knelt in prayer. Seeking the face of their Heavenly Father, they wander through their hearts and minds looking for some reason that He won't receive them. They let the past be the most important thing in their hearts. The Lord asks us to think on the good things, the heavenly, the holy, the righteous, not the filth that may plague our pasts.

The word repent simply means a change of mind. As you kneel to pray, repent of your sins, change your mind and think about God for awhile. His love for you is unconditional. As you approach the Throne, go boldly, don't look back. Don't wander into the Holy of Holies walking backward in fear of what lies behind. God loves you, let your thoughts remain on Him for the moment. Let His heart replace the fear and doubt.

You will never find tomorrow, if you spend all day today looking into yesterday. Walk on, eyes forward, and look for the hope of tomorrow as you come to the throne.

16 November 1991

I challenge you as you learn to forgive, stop walking through ice looking for something which never was and never can be. Look instead for all the hope God has for you. Look up Jeremiah 29:11 and find the Right Thoughts God has for you.

What is the Holy Spirit saying to you right now?

What thoughts are you being asked to replace?

What thought has the Holy Spirit just whispered to you about the way He sees you?

How does He want you to think about Him, you and you assignment to bless others?

How does this exercise impact your vision of the future and your place in it?

WHO YOU HURT

Few things are as difficult to carry as the burden of revelation of the pain you are responsible for causing others.

One of the greatest victims of your mistakes, harmful behavior and destructive choices is you. Your choices and addiction have hurt your future, your calling, your friends, your family and your reputation. Forgiving you will probably be the hardest act of contrition in your healing process.

Understanding this does not mean you have no work to do in the reconciliation of relationships of both victims and perpetrators of the past. In fact, it should inspire a greater motivation in you to seek forgiveness and to offer it.

When you see the pain victimization has brought in your life and the limiting beliefs which follow, then compare those to the pain and anxiety a lack of forgiveness brings, your heart should be broken for those who hold on to the pain you introduced them to. The need for release is tremendous.

There is more at play here than the way you feel. There is a chance you have emotionally wounded someone and you are not even aware of their pain. Your lack of awareness may be the most painful thing they have to endure.

This may also cause them to hold it against you spiritually and emotionally, perhaps even subconsciously. In this case, their hard feelings toward you, the angst they experience when you are around or even when you come to their mind, could easily become any one of numerous stress disorders or chronic diseases, in your life or in theirs. Remember, Dr. Leaf tells us 75-98% of chronic diseases in your body are caused by toxic thoughts.

This might seem a bit convoluted or complicated, but stay with me. Your ability to not hold against them, the bitterness they have toward you, will be one of the most healing decisions you can make in your life. I recently watched a movie where one of the characters was trying to reconcile with his ex-girlfriend. While in the midst of a heated discussion he uttered the words, "I forgive you!" Her anger was overwhelming. Obviously, they each had a different view of what happened and who was to blame. I am sure there have been times in my life when I hurt someone but really wanted an apology from them because of the way they responded to my carelessness. Is there any chance that is true for you?

You need to reconcile your feelings and emotions with your actions in order to experience forgiveness. You need to comprehend the depth of impact your behavior has had on others. You need to realize, you may never see have the opportunity to express your remorse, to sooth the pain you have caused, to erase the scars you have left behind. You need to be aware of reality.

Many people who experience trauma at the hands of another will spend the rest of their living days hating, seething, regretting, wishing ill, cursing and despising the perpetrator. No amount of begging, apology, explanation, contrition, or remove will change the condition of their wounded heart. You cannot make it right again.

As heartless as it seems, this is the place where you must forgive those who you have hurt in order to move forward in your own healing and freedom. If you will not release their bitterness, they will own you for the rest of your life. If you will not forgive the hatred they have expressed toward you in word or deed, you will not find peace. Once you have acknowledged the depth and breadth of your sin and the pain you have inflicted on them, your request for forgiveness from them (if the Holy Spirit tells you to ask), should be immediately followed by you forgiving them for what they cannot let go. Regardless their response to you, hatred or forgiveness, you must forgive.

SUMMARY & ACTION

There is nothing in this world or the next more powerful than forgiveness. I have experienced the life transforming power of grace. I know the work the Holy Spirit has done in my life, my mind, my heart, my spirit and I know none of it could have occurred if the bondage of sin still held me captive. As a slave to sin, my master wanted nothing less than total annihilation. He wants nothing less for you.

Your failure to forgive is a prison where the slave master keeps you in chains. As long as you choose not to forgive, you choose to remain a slave. As long as you hold bitterness and regret against yourself, those who have victimized you and those who harbor resentment toward you, you are powerless to love as you have been loved.

The greatest commandment is this: "Love the Lord your God with all your heart, mind, soul and strength. The second one is like it: Love your neighbor as you love yourself."

When you lack forgiveness, you lack love. Pursue both.

FORGET

Forget, not as the inability to remember but as the choice not to recall.

SIN

Sin is a choice to follow temptation into destruction even when fully aware there is a high price to pay.

You know as well as I do, it is hard to be tempted to do something you have interest in. If there was no desire, there would be no temptation. If there was no temptation, sin would be simple to resist. You do not "fall into sin" that has no appeal to you. Would you agree?

Of course you do. So what does forgetting have to do with the sin of addiction? Everything! Because you choose to sin, you have created a series of responses to stimuli which are incredibly predictable. If your addiction is chocolate cake, your weakness will be quickly obvious. If your addiction is playing video games for hours on end, your weakness will also be obvious. If you have a habitual response to the stimulus of chocolate cake or video games, chances are you do not even think about your response to the stimulus, you simple react out of habit. When stimulated by your source of temptation, you pursue it until you find yourself in bondage to it again.

All of this activity happens in the recesses of the brain known as neuropathways. These pathways are engraved by your choices and habits. Things you think, actions you take, beliefs you hold on to and attitudes which drive your behavior all become part of your neuropathways. They also become thoughtless responses. These reactions or responses are subconscious, meaning you don't have to focus attention on these reactions for them to happen. They just happen as natural as breathing from emotional muscle memory.

When it comes to your addiction, your neuropathways have been trained, carved, engraved to respond to stimulus the same way every time, because its what you have always done.

To break this cycle will require you to be intentional, to focus your attention, and to recognize these subconscious responses as early in the cycle as possible. This is the exact reason we started this book and this process with identifying the thoughts and actions in your life which absolutely must change.

You will not change what you do not identify as a problem. In order to change it, you will need to identify, make note, replace and then forget.

Forgetting is NOT a failure to remember, it is a choice not to recall, to dwell, to focus or to respond to past destructive stimulus. Breaking your addiction will be a matter of choosing to ignore stimulus. Truly, the hardest part of this choice is knowing sin is fun. Sad, but true, sin is fun. If it was not, you would not be tempted. Here in lies the challenge you must face.

Taking every thought captive means catching the stimulus on the way into your mind, identifying it as destructive, then forcing it to comply with the mind of Christ which is alive in you. Fasting is a great tool for the practice of forgetting. The mental discipline required for true fasting is a close match to the mental discipline needed to forget "how good sin once was."

Once in my life I fasted from everything but water for more than 30 days. After day eight, I literally forgot I was supposed to be hungry. The pangs of hunger were simply no longer there. I cannot explain it more than to say, I experienced a peaceful release of desires which once drove me. I found myself fascinated by the mealtime rituals of others, the amount of time spent snacking, "foraging" and cooking. In that season, I spent those times in deep meditation around a pool table, running, in the gym, or alone in the woods deep in worship.

Until you have fasted beyond ten days, the temptations of food and drink remain strong. The desire to eat, the habits of mealtime, the rituals associated with gathering over food will overwhelm you. You will physically feel sick and nauseas. You will emotionally feel drained, cranky and irritable. You will question your decision to fast. You will look for excuses to eat something. You will silently and prayerfully beg for a reason to break your fast. You will clearly remember how good food is to your tastebuds. You will long for the sensation of fullness in your belly. You will miss the people and fellowship of meals. You will realize how addicted you are to the process beyond gathering the nutrition needed to sustain your being. However, if you can persist in strength and discipline, you will forget you are hungry. Trust me, then verify for yourself.

In this process of fasting, you will be retraining neuropathways. You will be driving your mind, both conscious an subconscious into submission. Once you have tamed your mind and found the discipline needed to forget, your power over addiction will become clear and obvious. Hear me clearly on this, the ability and need for your body to submit to your mind, will and emotion is absolutely critical to your success in freedom. HOWEVER, do not expect your body to submit to a soul which is not submitted. You can change your life with discipline, fortitude and effort but transformation takes place ONLY when the mind is submitted to the Spirit of God in you.

List some of the stimuli in your life related to your addiction which cause you to react or respond without consciously thinking.

What thoughtless responsive actions do you find yourself engaged in with regard to these stimuli?

What stimulus do you need to forget or detach from response to by submitted mental discipline?

LIES

You have been lied to and the chances are high, the greatest liar in your life is you.

If you are honest with yourself, there are habitual actions and reactions in your life based on facts which you know to be untrue. An example might be the reaction of your spouse when you don't get your way. Perhaps your response is a dramatic over reaction and extremely exaggerated over generalization. "You never..." "You always..." "If you would just once time..."

These lies and others like them will drive your addiction into a place of selfish seclusion. These lies are the foundation of many decisions in your life. It's time to forget the lies. Stop repeating the lies. Pursue the truth which these lies have worked so hard for so long to hide. Forget the false comfort your lies have brought. Forget the false sense of security and self righteousness the lies have provided. Forget the reasoning, excuses, exaggerations, explanations and manipulations which created these lies to begin with. The lies you have told yourself, the lies others have told you and the lies you have told others all need to be eradicated and forgotten - choose to not recall and dwell on them.

What are the core lies which have driven your addiction?

BEHAVIORS

Some things just feel good to do them. This is no justification for continuing destructive behavior,

Whether fasting a particular food or all food, a particular habit or collective behavioral pattern, you must face the reality of why you do what you do. This brings us again to neuropathways. Behaviors are choices. Some behaviors are repetitive and habitual responses to subconscious thought. Some behaviors are clearly a choice consciously made in the moment. Some behaviors you choose because you enjoy the activity, the after effect, the result or the pleasure filled memories created, When these results are driving your choices of behavior more than the impact your behavior will have on others, you have a problem.

There are behaviors you will need to address the same way you have addressed lies and sin. Identify them as destructive and choose to replace them with other behavior. This will also require choosing not to remember the effects of the behavior you once craved. You will have to choose to not recall how good it feels to _____. Get high? Look at images you should not? Take that drink or shot or hit? These are your choices. These are your consequences to face. These are the memories you must sort and select based on the leading of the Holy Spirit. As your soul is submitted to the Holy Spirit you will begin to appreciate finer things, your appetites will shift, your desires will be altered, and your behavior should follow suit. What once drove you through craving will no longer have any appeal, but only if you choose to not recall the pleasure of the wicked enticement.

What enticements drive your behavior which you need to ignore?

How will you discipline yourself to forget the pleasing effects of destructive behavior?

What new behavior will you replace destructive behaviors with?

What new appetites have you experienced on this journey as you deepen your submission to the Holy Spirit?

WAY OF ESCAPE

Escape rooms are all the rage right now. Families choose to be locked in a small room and challenged to find a way out, Yes they par good money for this torture.

This section of the book is one the enemy will despise as much as any other because it is the key element of the mind puzzle of overcoming addiction and temptation. It has been said, "The Lord works in mysterious ways." I was marveling at this very statement in prayer more than two decades ago and the Holy Spirit whispered, "It's true you know."

As I stumbled in my thoughts to better understand, as a good teacher does, the Holy Spirit let me mentally rumble for a moment then continued the deeper explanation. He said, "The Lord does work in mysterious ways, but the devil will try ANYTHING!"

Forgetting the way of escape seems counter intuitive if you believe we should always know the "way out" of temptation to sin. We should always look for and identify the way out. However, we should not become so habitual and religious in our "way out" so as to become predictable.

Satan will try anything. If he senses we have spotted the snare, identified the trap, discovered the "exit ramp" he will add another trap we never expected. He will blindside us. He will destroy an opportunity. He will corrupt a relationship. He will bring in a new temptation which might even seem like a "good thing" or a gift from God. Predictability will also work against your own discipline and become its own form of temptation. Do you remember being a teenagers, raging with hormones? Do you remember the uncontrollable urges? Do you also remember how you would say to your date, "we will just kiss.' You both really truly believed you had this temptation thing figured out. You knew there was a "point of no return" beyond which your ability to resist was pointless.

Satan cannot see the future but he reads patterns really well and he has been doing it since before the creation of man. Satan knows your weaknesses, your point of no return and how to shift the moment. He will offer new opportunity and exaggerated stimulus to manipulate your escape route. Knowing when to say "no" seems so easy, but when the manifestation of sin doesn't follow the same path as before you could be trapped, then you're toast!

Forgetting the way of escape is about mental preparedness and mental discipline in the moment. I promise you Seal Team Six does not have one "trusty rusty escape plan" for every situation. In every combative environment the game changes. In every scenario you need a new plan.

As Napoleon once said, "The best battle plans ever drafted will not last past fifteen minutes of engagement with the enemy."

You need to have your spirit in tune. You need to have your soul (mind, will and emotions) trained like a Navy Seal to be aware of every hazard, every opportunity to escape, every weapon which is an asset and every potential threat. Do not rest on your past experiences, your best escapes from the past may never work again. Forget about it. Learn to be on the look out always for the next opportunity to win this skirmish, this battle, this combat engagement, then you will be equipped to always win the war.

What are your most common "ways of escape?"

What tried and true safety nets have you always relied on in the past?

Which ones have failed you when you were sure you were safe?

How can you sharpen your skills to always be on the look out for the way out?

What tools, weapons, assets can you identify to fight with against the worst temptation?

CONSEQUENCES

All too often the fear of consequences will stop us in our tracks from doing the right thing.

There are two reasons to forget the consequences. Remember we are talking about choosing not to recall, as opposed to failing to remember.

First, if you allow consequences to be your primary driver for behavioral modification, your motivation is wrong. If the enemy can temporarily blind others and allow you to "get away with it" long enough, your own arrogance will allow you to believe you always will. Relying on the magnitude of consequences as your leading deterrent will breed complacency, arrogance and false confidence. Loving one another through the consequences demands more of your relationship to be sure, but in the end, the honor and respect demonstrated through the process will pay huge dividends. Pay the price as needed. Face the reality of your addiction and your sin. Deal with what you must and trust loving mercy.

Second, while consequences are a strong negative reinforcement of behavior, consequences are like the bumper pads on the bowling lane. Consequences are needed for course correction when your behavior is off course or out of control. Learning to control your behavior, thoughts, and reactions, through submission and surrender is much more akin to learning to control the bowling ball through proper form, spin and lane position.

The value of your integrity and the power of transparency will reinforce love, grace, mercy and transformation significantly more than trying to avoid the consequences of your behavior through denial and deception. Facing the truth of who you are and which thoughts or feelings you permit to dominate your mind is the true journey to maturity.

If your battle against addiction can only be redirected after the fact through consequences, you are not yet experiencing the fruit of the Spirit in your life. Self control is a fruit of the Spirit. Self control is not a measured act of consequence avoidance. Self control is not a heightened exercise of self discipline. Self control is a matter of mature surrender to the Holy Spirit as he whispers to your soul.

> "The person who knows my commandments and keeps them, that's who loves me. And the person who loves me will be loved by my Father, and I will love him and make myself plain to him."
> John 14:21 MSG http://bible.com/97/jhn.14.21.msg.

Obedience requires more initiative than consequence avoidance. Obedience is the highest expression of love. Obedience is the hard work of mixing choice, intent and a soul surrendered to the will of the Father.

Be honest with yourself. Have you found your desire to overcome addiction driven more by the pain your consequences will bring to you than the love you have for the Father? Why?

Take a moment to speak a confession to Jesus, agree with him about the magnitude of His love's ability to transform you. Write your thoughts here. This conversation could be a life altering break through.

TRUTH

"A lie told once is a clearly a lie. A lie told a thousand times becomes truth."

You have experienced the reality of being deceived. How do I know? Because you are still reading! You have at one time bought into the lie which convinced you fulfillment would come through this addiction; your needs would be met, your heart would be satisfied, your cravings would be subdued. At this point you are realizing the power of deception and the hollow promises deception brings; but at some point you believed it all.

Forget the truth which is not truth at all. The greatest lie in all the world of humankind is to believe truth is subjective. The danger of believing in "your truth" as different from "my truth" cannot be overstated. It is the great foolishness of man to think truth can be "made up" or altered by man. We discussed the origin of absolute truth in previous chapters. If you are still wrestling with this reality of absolute truth, your journey to freedom may be truly impossible because without Him, you can do nothing.

"Jesus said, "I am the Road, also the Truth, also the Life. No one gets to the Father apart from me. If you really knew me, you would know my Father as well. From now on, you do know him. You've even seen him!""
John 14:6-7 MSG http://bible.com/97/jhn.14.6-7.msg

"But that's no life for you. You learned Christ! My assumption is that you have paid careful attention to him, been well instructed in the truth precisely as we have it in Jesus. Since, then, we do not have the excuse of ignorance, everything—and I do mean everything—connected with that old way of life has to go. It's rotten through and through. Get rid of it! And then take on an entirely new way of life—a God-fashioned life, a life renewed from the inside and working itself into your conduct as God accurately reproduces his character in you."
Ephesians 4:20-24 MSG http://bible.com/97/eph.4.20-24.msg

When I encourage you to forget truth, I am challenging you to forget everything you once believed to be true and to surrender to the inconvenient truth of Jesus Christ and his testimony of Himself and of the Father in Heaven. You will need to forget the lies about who you are: a victim; an addict; a hopeless, destructive, loser; a terrible friend; an unfaithful spouse; a failure as a parent. If you are redeemed by the blood, these things are the old you and are no longer true.

You need to learn to believe and receive what the Father says is true of you. You are loved, cherished, forgiven, healed, set free, empowered, a child of the King of Kings, a royal possession of the Kingdom of God, bought with a price and bought back from all you once were. You are a new creation in Christ. It is time to forget "your truth" and surrender yourself to His.

> "Jesus said, "You're not listening. Let me say it again. Unless a person submits to this original creation—the 'wind-hovering-over-the-water' creation, the invisible moving the visible, a baptism into a new life—it's not possible to enter God's kingdom. When you look at a baby, it's just that: a body you can look at and touch. But the person who takes shape within is formed by something you can't see and touch—the Spirit—and becomes a living spirit."
> John 3:5-6 MSG http://bible.com/97/jhn.3.5-6.msg

What truth do you need to let go of?

What truth do you need to lay hold of?

What promises have you received from the Father as an absolute truth?

REASON TO FIGHT

Most of your life you have been told "to fight is to fight against." It's time for a paradigm shift. Forget what you fight against and align yourself with the one who first fought for you!

In previous chapters, we discussed the need to define your motivation for overcoming your addiction. Do not think for one moment you can take your eyes off of those things if you still struggle on a daily basis against your addiction. In fact, if you have made it to this place in the book or seminar course and you are still wrestling and losing more often than winning, DO NOT LOSE HEART, but you should double down by starting over on page one and re-reading everything up to this point. No one goes to the gym one time to get in shape. No one studies martial arts one time and considers themselves a master. No one eats one meal and never gets hungry. The entire premise of this book is ICRFF - Identify. Confess. Repent. Forgive. Forget. Then rinse and repeat! Rinse and repeat is the key to success.

You might look around you right now and think, "Dagnabit, I am right where I was before." Look more closely. Chances are you are at the same position on the mountain (northwest corner/ 11 o' clock) but a significantly higher level than when you started this journey with me.

In the next pass, you are destined to discover your reason for fighting, your method for fighting, your motivation for fighting has shifted. Sure, writing this book has been cathartic for me however, YOU ARE the reason I fight now. YOU ARE what keeps me writing. YOU ARE my motivation. Your freedom is what I am fighting for now.

You too will one day see the liberty from your addiction and realize "I am secure in my surrender, now I know how to help others get free." You will begin to link arm in arm with other Victorious Warriors and charge the gates of Hell where we will not be overcome!

Feel free to choose not to remember everything you fought against. Forget the consequences you dreaded. Forget the losses you envisioned. Forget the pain which brought you to your knees to begin this journey in the first place. Look up new creature. YOU are a force to be reckoned with and all of Hell knows you by name.

Make a list of those you are standing in the gap for right here, right now.

WRONG THOUGHTS

You will get more of what you focus on most of the time.

Neuroscience has been hijacked in many areas and your thought life is one of them. From attitude to law of attraction, the system of this world has laid claim to truths only God the Father can take credit for. These realities have been laid at the altar of "universal consciousness" and "positive mental attitude." There is a word for such thinking, hogwash!

You will get what you think about most of the time because God will not be mocked. Whatever you sow, you're going to reap! If you think about failure most of the time, you will get failure. If you think about sin, addiction, pain, misfortune, victim hood - yes, you will get all of them and then some. Remember every seed contains the DNA to reproduce thousands of seed.

You need to go to the next level of repentance. You have already looked into every thought and reconciled it to what God thinks about it. It's time to remove the constant conscious awareness of sinful thinking from your mental menu. It's time to choose to not recall the wrong thoughts which brought you to the place of your addiction.

The thoughts which convinced you of your lack of worth need to go. The thoughts which told you there was no hope of freedom, forget them. The thoughts of past behavior and temptation which sneak into your dreams at night, choose not to recall. Do not entertain any thought which cannot be placed on the Mercy Seat as an offering.

What are some of those fleeting thoughts and vain imaginations which need to be cast down from your mental menu?

What are you thinking right this second? Write it down. On the next cycle through this process you will be fascinated to see how much your thinking has matured in surrender.

RIGHT THOUGHTS

The thinking which got you to where you are now will not get you to the next level.

Surely your thinking has evolved since we started this journey together. Surely your "righting thinking" has matured, deepened, become enlightened and reached a new level of expression. I am both excited for you and proud of you. But you're not done yet. I am about to hand you off. I have been your guide and your mentor for the time it has taken you to get here. My work is nearly done, yours is just beginning.

When Jesus vanished into the clouds an angel appeared and spoke to the astonished disciples. The angel's question is the question I leave you with as we wrap up our journey together.

> "These were his last words. As they watched, he was taken up and disappeared in a cloud. They stood there, staring into the empty sky. Suddenly two men appeared—in white robes! They said, "You Galileans!—why do you just stand here looking up at an empty sky? This very Jesus who was taken up from among you to heaven will come as certainly—and mysteriously—as he left.""
> Acts 1:9-11 MSG http://bible.com/97/act.1.9-11.msg

""I've told you these things to prepare you for rough times ahead. They are going to throw you out of the meeting places. There will even come a time when anyone who kills you will think he's doing God a favor. They will do these things because they never really understood the Father. I've told you these things so that when the time comes and they start in on you, you'll be well-warned and ready for them. "I didn't tell you this earlier because I was with you every day. But now I am on my way to the One who sent me. Not one of you has asked, 'Where are you going?' Instead, the longer I've talked, the sadder you've become. So let me say it again, this truth: It's better for you that I leave. If I don't leave, the Friend won't come. But if I go, I'll send him to you."
John 16:4-7 MSG http://bible.com/97/jhn.16.4-7.msg

"Then he said, "Everything I told you while I was with you comes to this: All the things written about me in the Law of Moses, in the Prophets, and in the Psalms have to be fulfilled." He went on to open their understanding of the Word of God, showing them how to read their Bibles this way. He said, "You can see now how it is written that the Messiah suffers, rises from the dead on the third day, and then a total life-change through the forgiveness of sins is proclaimed in his name to all nations—starting from here, from Jerusalem! You're the first to hear and see it. You're the witnesses. What comes next is very important: I am sending what my Father promised to you, so stay here in the city until he arrives, until you're equipped with power from on high."

SOLID ROCK CHRISTIAN FELLOWSHIP

He then led them out of the city over to Bethany. Raising his hands he blessed them, and while blessing them, took his leave, being carried up to heaven.

And they were on their knees, worshiping him. They returned to Jerusalem bursting with joy. They spent all their time in the Temple praising God. Yes."
Luke 24:44-53 MSG
http://bible.com/97/luk.24.44-53.msg

""You've heard me tell you, 'I'm going away, and I'm coming back.' If you loved me, you would be glad that I'm on my way to the Father because the Father is the goal and purpose of my life."
John 14:28 MSG http://bible.com/97/jhn.14.28.msg

""But my purpose is not to get your vote, and not to appeal to mere human testimony. I'm speaking to you this way so that you will be saved. John was a torch, blazing and bright, and you were glad enough to dance for an hour or so in his bright light. But the witness that really confirms me far exceeds John's witness. It's the work the Father gave me to complete. These very tasks, as I go about completing them, confirm that the Father, in fact, sent me. The Father who sent me, confirmed me. And you missed it. You never heard his voice, you never saw his appearance. There is nothing left in your memory of his Message because you do not take his Messenger seriously."
John 5:34-38 MSG http://bible.com/97/jhn.5.34-38.msg

It is time to shift your purpose, your thinking, your reason to fight, your surrender, your voice. You are witnesses to the power of God to transform a life. You are not the same person you were when we started. Your power, your wisdom, your understanding, your knowledge of the Holy Spirit are all deeper now and so is your calling and responsibility.

It's time to be led by the Spirit in a new and powerful way. Your best thinking will not get you to next. Only His thinking will get you there.

> "I was unsure of how to go about this, and felt totally inadequate—I was scared to death, if you want the truth of it—and so nothing I said could have impressed you or anyone else. But the Message came through anyway. God's Spirit and God's power did it, which made it clear that your life of faith is a response to God's power, not to some fancy mental or emotional footwork by me or anyone else.
>
> We, of course, have plenty of wisdom to pass on to you once you get your feet on firm spiritual ground, but it's not popular wisdom, the fashionable wisdom of high-priced experts that will be out-of-date in a year or so. God's wisdom is something mysterious that goes deep into the interior of his purposes. You don't find it lying around on the surface. It's not the latest message, but more like the oldest—what God determined as the way to bring out his best in us, long before we ever arrived on the scene. The experts of our day haven't a clue about what this eternal plan is. If they had, they wouldn't have killed the Master of the God-designed life on a cross. That's why we have this

205

Scripture text: No one's ever seen or heard anything like this, Never so much as imagined anything quite like it— What God has arranged for those who love him. But you've seen and heard it because God by his Spirit has brought it all out into the open before you. The Spirit, not content to flit around on the surface, dives into the depths of God, and brings out what God planned all along. Who ever knows what you're thinking and planning except you yourself? The same with God—except that he not only knows what he's thinking, but he lets us in on it. God offers a full report on the gifts of life and salvation that he is giving us. We don't have to rely on the world's guesses and opinions. We didn't learn this by reading books or going to school; we learned it from God, who taught us person-to-person through Jesus, and we're passing it on to you in the same firsthand, personal way."
1 Corinthians 2:3-13 MSG http://bible.com/97/1co. 2.3-13.msg

You are now a Victorious Warrior with people to help rescue. Like a spiritual Navy Seal, you need to be on the look out for injured souls. You need to be aware of the schemes of the evil one. You need to listen closely for the whisper of the Holy Spirit and practice implicit, immediate obedience. Your thoughts, your ways, your practices, your knowledge and your experiences are not enough. You are now a soldier in a war which is way over your head.

Engage with the Holy Spirit before you engage in any battle. Engage in scripture reading, fasting, prayer, surrender of will and pursuit of excellence before you engage in teaching, leading, coaching, training or ministry. Malcolm Gladwell says it takes an investment of 10,000 hours of preparation added to innate gifting to be considered an expert. If you are focused on spiritual growth at the same pace as a full time job (40 hours a week/ 2,080 hours per year) it will take you five years to become an expert.

How will you prepare yourself to match your gifting and calling?

What disciplines will you boost or adopt to be ready for warrior rescue?

Mountain climbers prepare for months before they arrive at base camp. What will your preparation look like?

WHO YOU HURT

Regret is easily a more vicious slave master than your worst failure.

There will be moments in your near future which demand clarity of thought and focus of purpose. In those moments, the greatest weapon of the enemy is to attack your self confidence. He will attack very effectively through reminding you of all you have done wrong. Satan need not get you on your knees worshiping him to defeat your purpose in Christ. He need only distract you. If you will simply take your eyes off of your victory to look back on your mistakes and the pain you have caused, he wins. Do you remember the old sophomoric game "made you look?"

Your ability to move in your calling, to hear the voice of the Holy Spirit, to move as God leads, to surrender your will to His plan all hinge on the power of your focused attention. As soon as the deceiver cries out "made you look" you have lost ground. I know where he likes to "make me look" and I know he will use the same tactic with you. He used it against David, against Paul, against Peter with great effectiveness. Carman mentions the enemy's strategy in a great song, "Revival in the Land." Look up the lyrics for great inspiration.

I know the battle you are fighting. I fought it. I know the future you are longing for. I am living it. I know the power you are up against. I faced it. I know He that is in you is greater. He is in me too. You are victorious through His victory. You will have to choose daily to not recall the people you have hurt. I know this seems calloused, but you will never fight like you were made to if the timidity of guilt is hanging over your soul.

The Father sees them. He knows how to love them, to restore them, to release them, to forgive them. No matter who you have hurt, The Father loves them more than you know how. Your recollection of the pain you caused serves no one but the enemy. If you have followed the steps in this book up to this point, you should choose to move on and allow God to do His part in their life. You have work to do.

SUMMARY & ACTION

We are here at the end of this cycle of the journey. You are not done. You are just beginning. Your calling is exposed and empowered up in this Victorious Warrior's journey.

Please take time to ask The Father about your next move. He has a plan for you or you would not be reading this page. I may have never seen your face. I may have never heard your voice, touched your hand, read an email message from you or whispered your name, but I love you and I am praying over you even now. I know there is an organization with the official name Orphan Rescue and I honor the work they do. I also know orphan rescue is the calling of everyone purchased by the blood of Christ. It is my calling and your calling to "seek and to save the lost" by introducing them to Jesus Christ.

Satan must have feared you severely to exert so much effort to destroy you. He must have read the patterns and trembled at the very thought of you taking on the world, surrendered to the Holy Spirit. This is all the more reason to speak up against his unlawful imprisonment of others. They too are more than victims, they are Victorious Warriors in the making. It's time we do the work we were called to do. I will ask Isaiah to close out this book with the reminder of your created reason for existence:

"GOD's Message, the God who created the cosmos, stretched out the skies, laid out the earth and all that grows from it, Who breathes life into earth's people, makes them alive with his own life: "I am GOD. I have called you to live right and well. I have taken responsibility for you, kept you safe. I have set you among my people to bind them to me, and provided you as a lighthouse to the nations, To make a start at bringing people into the open, into light: opening blind eyes, releasing prisoners from dungeons, emptying the dark prisons. I am GOD. That's my name. I don't franchise my glory, don't endorse the no-god idols. Take note: The earlier predictions of judgment have been fulfilled. I'm announcing the new salvation work. Before it bursts on the scene, I'm telling you all about it.""

Isaiah 42:5-9 MSG http://bible.com/97/isa.42.5-9.msg

God bless you. Get busy!!

TESTIMONY & BIO

My nightmare began when I was nine years old at a group sleep over when I was molested by an older boy. It was like an introduction to chocolate or gummy bears or liquor. I had no idea why it felt good. I had no idea where this open door would lead in my life. I just knew what happened felt good to me and I wanted more.

I spent the next two decades searching for more of those feelings. The opportunity to gratify my desire was a driving force in so many relationships and encounters. My heart was broken. My mind was broken. I had no hope for anything different. I didn't want anything different. I wanted a sexual fix, more sex.

My bedroom was littered with stolen magazines and posters of nude women. When I was home alone, I would search for all the explicit movies on the premium channels. There were "off market" videos and conversations and chance encounters with people twice my age and more sex. There were long term relationships destroyed by an insatiable craving for more sex. There was unfaithfulness, and more pain, and more sex.

There was no shortage of people who were curious, or addicts themselves. If I wanted sex, I was usually able to meet the need some way. I could sweet talk, or say just the right thing to create an opportunity within minutes with the right person. Girlfriends or strangers, it didn't matter. I would get a feel for how willing they were and decide to make a move, or simply ask. If there was no sexual interest, I would move on. For a season of my life, there were several partners who were willing and actively engaged in my sexual addiction, each of them knew about each other. All of them knew which one was "my girlfriend," but they were sexually involved on a regular basis anyway.

I recall one long term relationship where I revealed that I had been unfaithful and she said, "I can believe that. You have more 'love' than any one woman can handle."

There was enough pressure from the "normal people" that I had to hide my desires and cravings in the crevices of my mind. I tried to act out so many of the things I had seen and read about until I ran out of willing participants. I began to fantasize about encounters until I made them real in my mind so I could feel all the anxiety, the rush of emotions, the fear, the tantalizing excitement and release. Some memories and imaginations began to run together. I remember someone asking me if I bought a certain magazine or video and my reply was "I have already done more erotic things than they are willing to publish. Why waste the money? All I have to do is remember."

In the early days of sexual conquest, my cohorts and I would look for attractive single moms as ideal one night stands. We would often joke their kids were trophies to prove they were good in bed. In all, I had close to two dozen sexual partners. The stories were similar every time. It was an easy pattern to recognize. The scars of abuse, neglect, and sexual exposure were like beacons to me. I could spot fellow journeyers quite well, but the older I got, the deeper the expectations of a real relationship became. Women wanted more than a one night stand or a casual relationship. I thought if I just got married, I would have a willing partner all the time. She won't say no because she loves me. She will be willing to do anything I want.

I fell in love at first sight, but it may have been more about lust than love. When I arrived at the front door, the porch light was out and the living room light behind her lit up her silhouette through the thin white pant suit. Her form was stunning! Her rich blue eyes smiled at me and she welcomed me into her home. I was absolutely taken. Then all the signals became obvious. She was a single mom. She was recently divorced. She was living alone in a new city. She was far from home and starting her life over. PERFECT.

Over the next few months, I said all the right things and made all the right moves. I took her to church. I bought her small gifts. I mowed her yard. I was working harder in this relationship than ever before. "It better be worth it," I thought. Then I discovered in one of those long, late night conversations that she had been a victim of a date rape.

215

I felt a very strange emotional reaction to this revelation. Something weird started to happen in me. I was hurting for her. She was suddenly more than an exploit or sexual conquest. She was one of a kind to me. The first rape survivor I had ever spent time with. But she was also fellow traveler whose life had been forever redirected by a sexual encounter. I asked her to marry me.

I had sabotaged every relationship up too this point. I wanted to be loved, but not as much as I wanted sex. I also hated me so much for all the things I had done, I really did not feel like I was worthy of being loved and I was convinced no one wanted to be in a real relationship with someone like me. If she knew everything, she would be nuts to agree to marry me. She did.

On our wedding night there were no spectacular fireworks. We had dinner, sat for a while in the dining room and went back to the room. My heart was racing with anxiety and excitement. My expectations were so high, no porn star on earth could have been passionate enough for my desires. I had a wife now, not a sexual goddess who lived to fulfill my every sexual desire. Sure, she was hot and looked great behind closed doors. She loved me and gave me undivided and fully devoted attention, but I wanted more; more sex, more new experiences, more fulfilled fantasies, more pornography, and more sex.

She was living my nightmare now. I asked, pleaded, requested, cajoled, manipulated, bargained, begged and even cried to get what I wanted in the bedroom. I had this incredible belief that somehow she would one day "awaken" to the passion and excitement and learn to crave sex in the same way. I wanted her to want me as much as I wanted sex. It was torture to both of us. My demands on her were unrealistic and painful. Her self restraint was for her own protection, but felt like a cold shoulder to me. My self restraint was nonexistent.

Then came the internet and another depth of addiction. An opportunity to hide the craving, yet meet the need was perfect. I could have every fantasy I had ever imagined. All I had to do was search the right terms and someone had already done it and caught it all on video. That's when I really became a slave. A spark of imagination, an idea of a "new experience" would open a whole new level of sexual experiences I had never pondered. Notions that would once turn my stomach began to turn me on. Desires I knew I would never enjoy became the very thing I sought out. I would look at myself in the mirror and wonder who I had become, but the cravings were so strong, so deep, so dark I pursued them anyway. I tried to meet the need for more. I tried to quit. I tried to meet the need for more. I tried to quit. What a horrible cycle of torture and pleasure, of guilt, shame and enjoyment. I was a wreck.

One day, as a married father of four, I was in the shower, doing what sex addicts do, and my three year old son who liked to sleep in the shower at my feet, woke up. He caught me in the act. In his precious little voice he said, "Dad, can we be done now?" In that moment, I was annoyed.

In the next few months, I would begin a whole new level of struggle. I had been sitting in the church, teaching in the church, reading the Bible to my kids, and living with this addiction all at the same time. The revelation hit me like a freight train, my wife thought she married a "man of God" but she married me, an addict, a slave to sexual sin. If I did not hate myself before, I did now. At a men's meeting as the leader spoke about "putting away childish things" I heard a whisper. "What if someone else was doing that I was doing in the shower and made my son watch?" and I thought I would rip their arms off and beat them to death with them. Then the voice whispered, "You are that man."

I was broken. It was time to make a permanent change. I had prayed for forgiveness. I had asked for people to forgive me for what I had done with them. I had begged God to give me power to fight the temptation, but I was still a slave. If the slave master of sexual addiction spoke, I answered. I responded to every temptation. I gave in to every lustful notion or feeling. It was destroying everything and everyone I had come to love. I was sick and tired of it.

Nothing is was as dark as the prison of my own mind. Even now I look back at the places I have been in my imagination and it makes me cringe. The power of addiction is a destructive force. Everything I thought and believed was a lie. The bondage was horrendous, the shame unbearable, the guilt perpetually haunting and the fear of being found out owned me. The exposure to sexuality when my heart and mind were too young to comprehend the consequences devastated my ability to make good choices.

Now it was time to fight back. I joined a class at church which truly attacked the issue of sexual sin head on. We worked through a book which was direct, heartfelt and written with passion to win. One day in class, I had a vision of myself hanging over the Grand Canyon staring at the darkness below the sun line. I was leaning out over the abyss and trembling in fear. The only thing holding me back was a shoestring of grace. The whisper said, "You have no idea what lies in that darkness. It contains every sexual sin you have not yet experienced. If you stay in this addiction, those things will utterly destroy you in every sense. Get off this path and do it now."

A few weeks later, I was given another vision. I saw a huge buffet table. From left to right I saw lines of cocaine, a pile of cash, a bottle of liquor, a pecan pie and a naked woman. The whisper said, "Which one would you fight me for?" I replied, "I have never been high in my life, keep the cocaine. I am not driven by money, keep the cash. I have never been drunk, keep the liquor. Now I might fight you for the pecan pie and the woman… that's a tough choice." The whisper replied, "That's your problem. When you want ME more than you want those things, then you will be free."

It has been more than a decade since that conversation. I have found strength in unusual places to resist temptation. I have fought battles with and for friends, family and strangers who fight against addiction. I have seen the incredible impact that pornography has on marriages, children and society at large.

We are sadly beginning to see a cultural shift to make sexuality and the use of pornography publicly acceptable and publicly accessible. I cannot tell you how much that hurts my heart. Young people are getting married at a lower rate, because internet pornography and open sexuality no longer require a committed relationship for sexual expression. The average age of exposure to explicit imagery is nine years old. The number of people who are addicted to pornography and do not consider it a problem would boggle the mind. I recently saw a study which stated, a higher percentage of millennials consider littering morally wrong than consider pornography morally wrong. Young people are not only exposed to sexually explicit images in dark places. These images are found in text books, social media, billboards and basic prime time television. Premium channels and on demand video are also portals into the home that leave young people at risk.

I know that beyond my own foolishness, some of my own children have been exposed to sexuality long before it was the right time of their life. My wife and I are both very aware of the impact of sexual desires run amuck. We have experienced it first hand and we know how it destroys families. It is my hope for the truth of the impact of pornography and sexual addiction to be exposed for the danger and harm they really are and for the light of Jesus Christ to shine in the dark places to reveal hope for freedom.

There are news stories everyday of public figures, ministers, athletes, professionals who are incarcerated, exposed and destroyed because the addiction has won. If you are struggling with this addiction, please get help before it robs you of everything important. There is hope and power in the name of Jesus Christ. Those who are His, have overcome, because He has been tested and tempted in everyday and yet was without sin. If He lives in you, you have the same power. Find a mentor, find a pastor, find hope!

J Loren Norris and Karin live in Cedar Hill, Texas. Karin has a B.S. in Psychology and Loren is a Certified Leadership Coach and a Founding Partner of the John Maxwell Team. Loren has traveled across the US and internationally to places like Congo DRC, Brazil, Honduras, Cuba and England as a speaker and leadership trainer. Loren also provides personal development and leadership training globally via Facebook Live video on a daily basis and is in recording and production for a brand new Christian talk show called *Meet The Messenger*.

Together, Loren and Karin host seminars and study groups, speak at conferences and interview fascinating couples for *Transforming Grace TV*.

Karin released *5 Battle Positions of a HAPPY Wife* in 2016. Loren is the author of *Live A More Excellent Life, God At Work, 5 Battle Strategies of A Victorious Warrior* study guide, *Attitude Hack, Learn To R.O.A.R. Leadership* and *Learn to R.O.A.R. Communication*. (All available on Amazon)

Loren and Karin are available to speak and train individually or as a team. You can get more information and contact them at www.TransformingGrace.Tv.

PRAYER OF SALVATION

Heavenly Father, I come to You in the Name of Your Son Jesus Christ. You said in Your Word that whosoever shall call upon the name of the Lord shall be saved. (Romans 10:13) Father, I am calling on Jesus right now. I believe He died on the cross for my sins, that He was raised from the dead on the third day, and He's alive right now. Lord Jesus, I am asking You now, come into my heart. Live Your life in me and through me. I repent of my sins and surrender myself totally and completely to You. Heavenly Father, by faith I now confess Jesus Christ as my new Lord and from this day forward, I dedicate my life to serving Him.

In Jesus Name,

Amen.

SOLID ROCK CHRISTIAN FELLOWSHIP

77103993R00124

Made in the USA
Columbia, SC
22 September 2017